SAMI POTATOES

LIVING WITH REINDEER AND PERESTROIKA

Michael P. Robinson and Karim–Aly S. Kassam

Linguistic Editor: Leif Rantala

Bayeux *Arts*

Published in 1998 by
Bayeux Arts, Inc.
119 Stratton Crescent S.W.
Calgary, Canada T3H 1T7

Visit our Website: www.bayeux.com

Design by Brian Dyson
Copy editing by Luisa Alexander Izzo
Photographs on page 51 by Terry Garvin
Works by John Andreas Savio courtesy of the Savio-museet, Kirkenes, Norway
Eighteenth-century etchings from *Beskrivelse over Finmarkens Lapper* (1767)
by Knud Leems

Canadian Cataloguing in Publication Data
Robinson, Michael P.
  Sami potatoes

Includes bibliographical references and index.
ISBN 1-896209-21-1 (bound) 1-896209-11-4 (pbk.)

1. Sami (European peoples)—Social conditions.
2. Sami (European peoples)—Economic conditions.
I. Kassam, Karim-Aly S., 1964-. II. Rantala, Leif. III. Title.
DL42.L36R62 1998   306'.0899455   C98-910689-6

 The Arctic Institute of North America acknowledges the
support of the University of Calgary – Gorbachev Foundation
in the conduct of this work.

Bayeux Arts gratefully acknowledges the support of the Canada Council
for the Arts and the Alberta Foundation for the Arts for its publishing programme.

Frontispiece
John Andreas Savio, Alone, *woodcut, 19cm x 26.5cm*

Printed in Canada

An eighteenth-century drawing of reindeer migration (Leems, 1767).

In memory of
Matryona and Valery Sotkoyarvi of Jona,
and for the Sami of Lovozero and Jona,
who continue the struggle to
protect their homeland.

TABLE OF CONTENTS

PREfACE

Sami Potatoes is the story of the Russian Sami Co-Management Project, which was initiated in 1995 by the Arctic Institute of North America, the Russian Kola Sami Association, and the Institute of Ethnology and Anthropology, Russian Academy of Sciences. The project was funded by the University of Calgary-Gorbachev Foundation, as one of its first initiatives. Its intent was to introduce the concept of natural resource co-management to Russia, using Canadian methodology and Russian research trainees. The project also sought to introduce Russia to participatory action research (or PAR), a process that focuses on training local people to conduct research of their choosing in their communities to meet their desired ends. From the start the Russian Sami, led by Kola Sami Association President Nina Afanas'eva, showed great enthusiasm for PAR, and the citizens of the main Sami communities of Lovozero and Jona now have the tools to practise co-management in their homelands. Just what these tools are and how they were developed is the subject of this book.

There would have been no Sami Co-Management Project without the idea for its creation: that idea was the gift of Lloyd Binder and Nina Afanas'eva, who met in 1994 in Kiruna, Sweden, to discuss potential joint projects between Russia and Canada. Lloyd is the maternal grandson of Mikkel Pulk, a Sami

Lloyd Binder and Michael Robinson with Nina Afanas'eva in Lovozero.

The children of Jona with Nina Afanas'eva and Lloyd Binder.

herder who journeyed from Norway to Alaska in 1929 to help drive a herd of 3,400 reindeer to the Canadian western Arctic, and to teach reindeer herding to the Inuvialuit.

One might ask why and how a Sami herder came to Canada with Alaskan reindeer in the early 1930s. The story began in Czarist Russia in 1892, when 171 reindeer were imported to Alaska from Siberia. In 1902, the Czar prohibited further exports, but by then 1,280 reindeer had been imported into Alaska. By the 1930s, some 600,000 reindeer were grazing the Alaskan tundra, and it was from this stock that the government of Canada had purchased its 3,400 animals in 1929. Canada needed the reindeer—and the Sami herding expertise of Mikkel Pulk and others—because commercial whaling in the Beaufort Sea was in steep decline, and coastal caribou herds were being severely depleted. The influenza epidemics of 1902 and 1918 had also taken their toll. For the Inuvialuit and Gwich'in of the Mackenzie delta region, life was becoming a struggle for survival. The Canadian government saw the introduction of Russian reindeer via Alaska as the solution to the problem (North, 1991).

With this historical background, it is perhaps understandable that Lloyd Binder, of Sami and Inuit parentage, would see a connection between Canada and Russia that centred on reindeer co-management. Both his Sami mother,

Ellen, and his Inuk father, Otto, have worked hard to keep the Inuit-Sami connection alive in Inuvik and the Kautokeino region of Norway. Lloyd was perfectly placed to see the potential next evolution in this cultural exchange, especially as an Inuvialuit comprehensive land-claim beneficiary with knowledge of Canada's oldest co-management regime. *Sami Potatoes* is indebted to his vision and to Nina Afanas'eva's persistence in the call for social justice for the Russian Sami.

CHAPTER I
INTRODUCTION

The Russian Sami, whose present-day struggle for cultural survival and land-use reform in the Kola Peninsula is the essence of this book, are the easternmost members of the Sami people, whose homelands also span the northern regions of Norway, Sweden, and Finland. Since the collapse of the Soviet state in the late 1980s, they have been blessed with the freedom to travel and meet with their Fennoscandian Sami neighbours, but cursed with the progressive dismantling and decay of state-supplied health care, pensions, farm employment, housing, and virtually all other forms of support from the old Soviet system. In the new era of openness and free enterprise, the Sami have been left to scramble for food, shelter, and their very dignity in an environmental landscape checkered with aging mines and smelters; atomic power stations; missile, submarine, and surface fleet bases; and three reported atomic waste storehouses. They are also faced with daily poaching of their remaining reindeer herds as the majority Russian population of their homeland also comes to grips with the pain of economic transition. The authors of this book have travelled to the Sami villages of the Kola, journeyed to the tundra, and worked collegially with a team of dedicated Sami community researchers to create a new basis for land-use reform and protective stewardship of the 60,000 reindeer that remain in nine brigade units organized under the Stalinist regime. A set of land-use and occupancy maps has been prepared in this process, for the first time in the Kola Peninsula. These maps show just how well the Sami know and use their land. The maps and the indigenous environmental knowledge that they contain provide the foundation for a new Murmansk County system of development project review and approval, based on the practical Canadian example of resource co-management. In essence, co-management is a process that enables scientists and indigenous experts to combine their knowledge and wisdom to take decisions about resource allocation and use. At its core, it enshrines the principle of the democratic intellect, the idea that both specialist and lay experts must combine their talents to take decisions for society and the common good.

   The conduct of this work involved many calculated risks. The University of Calgary- Gorbachev Foundation, though dedicated to easing the economic

An eighteenth-century drawing of a Sami boat sleigh (Leems, 1767).

and social transitions occurring in Russian society through joint Canadian/ Russian research initiatives, had no prior track record in the Kola Peninsula region. Thus it was immediately linked with Mr. Gorbachev himself, whom some Sami and ethnic Russian officials associate with the painful struggles of *glasnost* and *perestroika*. As well, many Murmansk County Administration

At Pavel's camp, July 1997.

Picnic on the tundra.

and elected Duma officials regarded the project as highly presumptuous and somewhat arrogant in its assumptions about Russian development. Who were we, as Canadians or Russian Sami, to question the abilities of the duly appointed and elected officials? Often we were reminded that Russia has survived for 800 years, and that Canada celebrated its first century only recently. Furthermore, why did Canadians from Calgary think they had any ideas about Russian society, or the Russian North? And did we all not fully appreciate that the County Administration did not consider the Kola Sami Association an "official organization"?

As Canadians, we took two years to understand fully the Russian visa and passport requirements. Many hours were spent in police stations and County Administration offices and at different border crossings explaining why we lacked permission to be in or to go to various Sami villages. It sometimes did not help, in 1995, that "Canadian" and "Chechin" could be pronounced nearly the same way. We often drove down long country roads past extraordinary military installations that seemed strangely out of place in the boreal forest or tundra, and we were reluctant to take photographs lest we be taken for spies. It was always unnerving to the Canadians to see openly brandished guns at military checkpoints, and to pass by miles of electrified border fencing adjacent to lakes dotted with children in sailboats.

However, as the project entered its third year, we grew more and more fond of Mother Russia, of our Sami partners and their indefatigable spirit, of Russian humour, of the achievements of the old Soviet state in the fields of education, science, industrial design, health care, and culture. We even learned to appreciate the checks and balances of Duma and Administration, the strong role of local government officials, and the frank expression of ideas in virtually any conversation. We learned also about the importance of maintaining communications with our partners through all possible media and the reliance civil discourse places upon trust, loyalty, and continuity. The human relationships forged by the Sami Co-Management Project are now lifelong friendships, as indicated by care and concern about our collective grandparents, parents, children, and friends, the annual exchange of Christmas cards and gifts, the continuous recall of humorous situations, our shared grief at the passing of elders and project participants, and our delight in the news of newborns.

A FEW WORDS ABOUT OUR METHODOLOGY

By now the reader may be wondering about the science and methodology we used in our work and the issues raised by training local people to do their own research. It may appear that the Sami Co-Management Project was more collegial than expert-driven, that the methodology was excessively participatory, and that replication and validation of results will prove difficult, if not impossible. Some will wonder about the whole concept of co-management, which at first may seem to be abdication of essential scientific standards. All of the above concerns are addressed in the following chapters, which combine and alternate narrative and expository text to tell the story. Some of what follows is excessively technical; some is historical, some is personal, some is journalistic, and some is traditional. *Sami Potatoes* has been written this way to challenge certain concepts of research, and to demonstrate the breadth of experience that truly participatory research projects are capable of generating.

While two Canadian authors have written the book, every word has been read back verbatim to our Sami partners. Our translator and linguistic editor, Leif Rantala, has also checked the text carefully, and we have attempted to make every correction that has been suggested on the basis of fact or Sami tradition. The maps included with the text were made by the Sami mapping teams in Lovozero and Jona, following a methodology developed in Canada and made relevant to the Russian context. Each map was validated by local Sami elders and reindeer herders in public, open-house sessions where researchers stood by their work to make corrections and additions of new data.

This work is printed in its entirety with the permission and blessing of the Kola Sami Association, and has already been publicly presented in Lovozero and Murmansk to elected officials, senior County administrators, and the media. Both the mayor of Lovozero, Mr. Nikolai Brylov, and the vice-governor of Murmansk County, Mr. Vasili Kalaida, have commended the mapping teams for their work and the potential future of co-management in the Kola. The stage has now been set for a new era of land-use planning in the Kola Peninsula: an era of planning that combines local knowledge with scientific expertise in the cause of land and resource stewardship.

An eighteenth-century drawing of Sami fishers (Leems, 1767).

CHAPTER 2
LAND, HISTORY, CULTURE, AND SURVIVAL:
THE KOLA PENINSULA AND THE RUSSIAN SAMI

The homeland of the Russian Sami is today officially known as the Murmansk Oblast (region) of Russia. Historically, this region has been referred to as Kola, and earlier as the Alexandrovskii district of the Archangelsk region; still others have referred to it as Russian Lapland or the Kola Peninsula (Volkov [1946], trans. Lasko and Taksami, 1996; Louk'yanchenko, 1994). Today just over 1,033,000 residents live on the Kola Peninsula (*Lapin Kansa*, April 12, 1997), and the 1989 Russian census put the Sami population at 1,600 people (Murmansk Region Committee of Statistics, 1995:5). Altogether, the Kola Peninsula contains 16 towns, 20 urban settlements, and 149 rural settlements.

Pavel Fefelov adjusting his tundra television.

Checking the nets on Lovozero Lake.

The largest towns, in order of population, are Murmansk (population 406,100 in 1995); Apatity (population 74,500 in 1995); and Monchegorsk (population 63,200 in 1995) (Murmansk Region Committee of Statistics, 1995:4). The main Sami community is Lovozero, a reindeer herding and cultural centre, which in 1997 was estimated to have 3,500 residents (Nikolai Brylov, Mayor of Lovozero, pers. comm. 1997), of whom 940 were Sami in 1995 (Kaminsky, 1996:150).

In 1994, reindeer herding was classified by the Murmansk Region Committee of Statistics (1995:13) as a component of "other" industry, easily outstripped in importance by the production of metals, foodstuffs, electricity, and mining chemicals, which account for 40, 22, 20, and 9 per cent, respectively, of industry output in the Murmansk Region. An indication of the importance of the Murmansk Oblast's industrial output to Russia are the facts that in 1994 the region produced 9.8 per cent of Russia's ferrous concentrate and 100 per cent of its apatite concentrate. In 1994 the Oblast's main trading partners were Norway, Finland, Germany, and Sweden (Murmansk Region Committee of Statistics, 1995:17).

Against this background of industrial-economy towns and a history of successive economic invasions of the North by ethnic Russians, Ukrainians, Belorussians, Tartars, Moldavians, Karelians, and others, the Sami struggle on in the 20th century with a culture that has roots in northern Finland and Karelia as well as in the Kola Peninsula (Louk'yanchenko, 1994:310). This culture first found expression in Russian history in 1216, when the Sami paid their first taxes to Russia. The first detailed ethnographic description of the Kola Sami was given by Nikolai Ozeretskovskii in *The Description of Kola and Astrakhan* (1804), as reported in N.N. Volkov's *The Russian Sami* (1946, trans. Lasko and Taksami, 1996:7). Significant articles by a variety of Russian, Finnish, and Norwegian academic authors followed; they too are ably summarized and evaluated in N.N. Volkov (1946, trans. Lasko and Taksami, 1996:7-11). These works detail archaeological research, material culture, fairy tales and myths, and speculation on Sami origins. Notably, it was not until the 1930s that Russian literature began to explore "the question of the former unity of ancient European culture and contemporary Sami culture" (Volkov [1946], trans. Lasko and Taksami, 1996:11).

Louk'yanchenko, writing in 1994 in the cultural encyclopedia *Narody*

PROJECT LOCATION

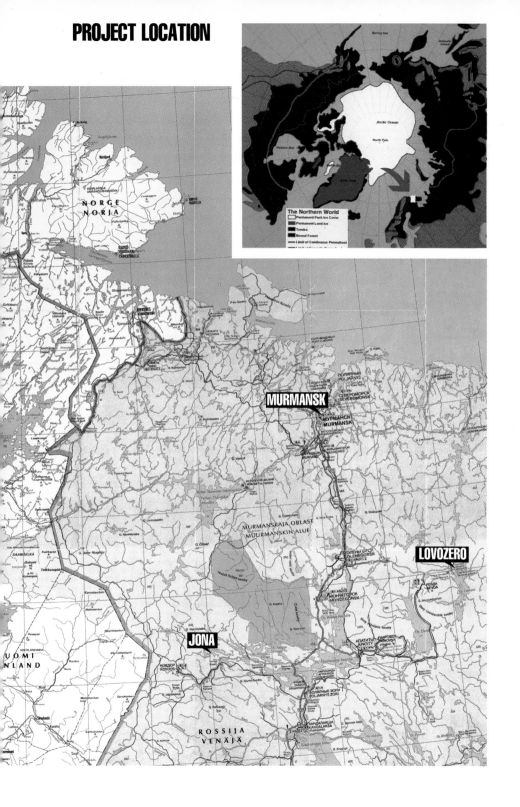

Rossii, reports four dialects for the Kola Sami—Jokanga, Kildin, Notozero, and Babino—and explains that 1,000 years ago, the Russian Sami ranged over a much larger area to the south and east than today. In the 16th and 17th centuries, the Kola Sami territory included parts of northern Karelia. By the end of the 19th century, the Sami had been forced north and had given up the southern part of the Kola region to ethnic Russians. At that time the centre of Sami culture in the Kola became Lovozero. The 1926 census of the Murmansk region reported 205 Sami residents in Lovozero; 338 in settlements on the Tuloma River to the northwest; 160 in Jokanga and 139 in Semiostrov, on the Barents Sea north coast; 105 in Voron'e, north of Lovozero and now under water because of power station development (Leif Rantala, pers. comm 1997); and 82 in Babinsk village, which was located near the present village of Jona (Volkov [1946], trans. Lasko and Taksami, 1996:6). All told, the 1926 census revealed a total of 1,582 Sami in over 16 settlements in the Murmansk Region. Today, 40 per cent of the Russian Sami live in towns, all know the Russian language, and over 50 per cent of Sami marriages are with people of other nationalities (Louk'yanchenko, 1994:310).

Louk'yanchenko theorizes (1994:310-311) that the old Sami culture, characterized by a mixture of hunting, fishing, and reindeer herding, began at the end of the first millennium A.D. Regional economic specialization occurred in the Kola Peninsula. The Sea Sami developed sophisticated techniques to harvest sea mammals, especially seals, and the central Kola Sami communities developed expertise in the fur harvest, specializing in arctic fox and beaver, and also in the harvest of wild reindeer, often using tame reindeer as living decoys. By the end of the 19th century, the wild species of animals, fish, and birds began to decline, and the Kola Sami refocused their efforts on reindeer herding, guiding for scientific parties, building railroads, and surveying new routes for roads (Louk'yanchenko, 1994:310-311). At the same time, starting in the late 1880s, the Komi and their Nenets herders entered the Kola Peninsula, fleeing a reindeer plague in their traditional homelands of the Pechora region near the Izhma River to the east. Volkov (1946, trans. Lasko and Taksami, 1996:123) reports that the Izhma culture of the Komi influenced the Sami to adopt a new, more intensive system of reindeer herding: the herders travelled with the reindeer all the time. Traditional Sami herding practices differed from those of the Komi and the

Nenets in that the Sami had smaller herd sizes, permitted free grazing of reindeer in the summer, used log barns and fences to contain animals when necessary, employed dogs for herd control, and built smudge fires to drive persistent mosquitoes away from the herds (Louk'yanchenko, 1994:310; members of the Lovozero and Jona mapping teams, pers. comm. 1996 and 1997).

Central to understanding Sami hopes for the future is a solid understanding that reindeer herding is still important today, even though fewer than 100 Sami herders continue to practise the craft, from the home base of the Tundra Joint Stock Reindeer Company in Lovozero. The Sami year still honours the cycle of seasonality dictated by herding, which is based on regenerating reindeer stock. Volkov (1946, trans. Lasko and Taksami, 1996:24-25) notes that fawning (also called calving) is the most important part of the cycle: it starts around May 10-15, and ends in early June.

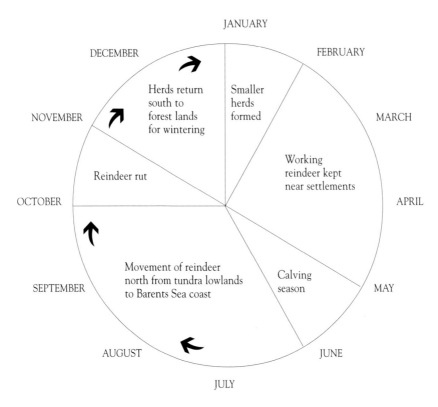

RUSSIAN SAMI SEASONAL ROUND

The town of Nikkel.

Successful calving requires protection from predators, quiet nursery areas, ample lichen, mild weather, and safe terrain for the newborns. The herders mark each calf at birth with a special identification nick (or mark) cut on its ears. In summer, the herds migrate northwards to the windy Barents Sea coast, to escape the hordes of mosquitoes and to graze on the best pastures, which offer grass, lichen, leaves, mushrooms, and cloudberry blossoms. On the coastal beaches, salt-sour grass and seaweed augment this diet. In the fall, from the end of September to the end of October, the reindeer rut takes place, as stags vie for dominance, and the evolutionary right to mate is established. After the rut is over, the herders gather the animals together and drive them back south to the forest lands above the tundra lowlands. In winter they divide the reindeer up into smaller herds, and keep the working reindeer near the Sami settlements, where they can be protected from wolves and other predators. Here they await spring, when the cycle begins once again with the onset of calving. The distinctive mobility of Sami society was keyed to this reindeer cycle, and the movements of the wild reindeer dictated the movements of the people.

By the end of the 19th century, there were 17 *siidas* (extended Sami family communities), each with its own territory for engaging in the annual round of activities. Special spring and fall locations existed for fishing and hunting. Winter localities were generally in the forest or close to the tree line, and close to good winter pasture. Summer camps were established on the shores

A Kola industrial wasteland.

of lakes, along rivers and streams, or on the seacoast. This distinctive form of land use and ownership covered almost the entire Kola Peninsula at the start of the 20th century, even though changes to accommodate the Komi and Nenets herding practices were under way.

A radical change for the Sami occurred in the 1920s, when the new Soviet state began to exert its influence in the Kola. To begin with, the state imposed its policy of compulsory reindeer harvests, which required the Sami to kill reindeer for the use of the Russians (Sarv, 1996:132- 133). Sarv reports a drastic decline in the reindeer population from 1914 to 1921; only about 40 per cent of the stocks survived that period. In 1928, the first collective farm was founded in the village of Voron'e. In the process, reindeer and Sami property were collectivized, and people who resisted were killed or exiled.

A second wave of collectivization, in 1933-41, led to further depredations and loss of Sami rights to land, water, and their nomadic lifestyle. All Sami lands were proclaimed the property of the Soviet Union, and those who opposed the reforms were brutally dealt with by the Stalinist purges. Sarv (1996:134) reports that the Sami village of Zapadnaya Litsa saw all of its men executed and all of its women and children deported.

While all of the above was occurring, the Soviet Union also launched an aggressive program of industrialization in the Kola Peninsula. Murmansk, Apatity, Monchegorsk, Olengorsk, Kovdor and other towns developed as government service centres, military bases, or mining and smelting communities. In 1920 there were about 14,000 inhabitants in the Kola Peninsula; by 1940, this figure had increased to 318,400. The Sami population in 1933 is reported to have been 1,800 (Sarv, 1996:133). Today's 2,000 Sami amount to only 0.16 per cent of the one million people living in the Kola region, and their number currently shows no sign of significant increase. In fact, Dr. V.I. Kaminsky, the chief physician of the Lovozero central hospital, notes that "the birth rate has been falling during the last few years, the natural growth rate is either zero or negative, and life expectancy is falling" (Kaminsky, 1996:156). For the Sami and their culture, living with reindeer in the era of *perestroika* has become a daily challenge to the human spirit. Unemployment, alcoholism, and anger are on the rise, and only life expectancy seems to be falling. For survival, a new reliance has been placed on the traditional livelihoods of reindeer herding, fishing, and hunting. And this very survival is challenged by the decades of Soviet abuse and neglect of the natural landscape. Sarv (1996:138) reports in consultation with Bellona (the Norwegian environmental non-governmental organization) that:

> ...two so-called peaceful atomic bombs have been detonated at Hiipine in 1974 and 1984. There are also three storage points for radioactive wastes on the Kola Peninsula as well as an atomic power plant with four reactors. Additional sources of waste are the 123 atomically powered craft and their bases along the coast. Industry has been the cause of extensive damage to forests and especially the Nikel and Monchegorsk areas.

Clearly the Sami, with their ancient and continuing relationship with the wild reindeer of the Kola Peninsula, are engaged in the greatest struggle possible—the struggle to preserve their culture, their land, their people, and their reindeer. That they persist at all in the face of their history in the Kola Peninsula is in itself remarkable. Their spirit of cultural survival and their actions to defend and protect their reindeer pastures and herds are of signal importance to us all.

CHAPTER 3
WHY SAMI POTATOES?

Why "Sami Potatoes"? Potatoes are to the Russians what wheat is to Canadians. Potatoes are the staple. The Russians have faced the vagaries of war and oppression by surviving on a diet of potatoes. The Sami have always derived their cultural and economic identities from reindeer herding. Sami potatoes are their reindeer. Reindeer herding is not only a livelihood or a source of income and food: it is a way of life. It is deeply embedded in the Sami psyche.

The title of our book emerged from a conversation with Andrei Gavrilov, a retired reindeer herder. As we began mapping the various birds, medicinal plants, trees, sacred sites, and traditional villages of the Kola Peninsula, we noted that from some hundred possible icons, our Sami partners chose to begin with the reindeer. Seeking an explanation for what in hindsight seems obvious, we asked Andrei why he chose to place the reindeer icons on the map first. He answered: "Because they are Sami potatoes!"

Andrei is not the typical reindeer herder. The signs of fatigue and stress are less strewn across his face. It has very little to do with his retirement. His pension is not sufficient to sustain him, and this is the reason why he is working on this project. There is a joie de vivre about him that catches us all in its embrace. It is refreshing, considering the sheer stress in the post-*perestroika* life of the average Russian, let alone the Sami. He injects poignant humour and we all laugh. His crisp response to our question is both a statement of fact and a plea for cultural survival. The subtle tension of Sami potatoes remains with us as we tell the story of the Kola Sami.

The reindeer is the metaphor of Sami spirituality: from it they derive meaning and express cultural symbols. The centrality of the reindeer in their lives is best demonstrated through the origin myth of Myandash, the Reindeer/man. This folk tale, typical of an oral culture, was traditionally sung by the Sami living east of Lovozero. It was first recorded by the Finnish linguist Arvid Genetz in 1876.

We relate this myth as it was told to us by Tat'yana Louk'yanchenko, the noted Russian ethnographer of the Sami, and Nadya Zolotuhina, a Sami schoolteacher in Lovozero. In the meantime, Andrei listens attentively.

Sami potatoes.

*What's good for the reindeer
is good for the Sami...*

Military fuel base on the Kirkenes-Murmansk road.

Once upon a time an elderly Sami couple had three daughters who had grown to womanhood, and the perennial question of marriage arose. In keeping with tradition, it was the eldest who had to marry first. The suitor of the first daughter was the Seal. He came to the cabin of her parents seeking her hand in marriage. Once married, the two moved to the sea home of the Seal. It was now the turn of the second daughter to get married. Her suitor was the Raven, who also approached the cabin of her parents to seek her hand. After their marriage, together they went to live in a nest in the forest. Finally, the youngest and the most beautiful of the daughters was ready for marriage. Her suitor was the Reindeer. Like the other two sisters, she also joined her husband, who lived in the tundra.

After some time, the parents began to notice an emptiness in their cabin because of the absence of their daughters. They decided that they would go and live with one of them. But first they would visit each of the daughters and see how they fared.

They began by visiting the first daughter, who lived far away by the sea. As they approached Seal's den, they were received by their grandchildren, who were half-human and half-seal. Together they entered the den, which was constructed from animal bones. To their horror, they found that their daughter was maimed and ill-treated by her husband. The Seal had eaten away the arms of his wife. The wife explained that he liked bone marrow. The parents, dismayed at the sad state of their first daughter, journeyed the next day to find their second daughter.

When they crossed into the forest they were received by the second set of grandchildren, who were half-human and half-raven. Together they approached the nest of the second daughter. It was a tangle of scraps and branches that were poorly kept. The parents' expectations of meeting their daughter in a joyous union with her husband were dashed when they saw that she had also been abused. The Raven had pecked out one of his wife's eyes. In fear of what might have happened to their third and favourite daughter, they quickly journeyed to meet her.

Upon their arrival in the tundra, they were met by their grandchildren, who were half-human and half-reindeer.[1] The third daughter came running out of her wooden cabin[2] to meet her parents, whom she was delighted to see. To their relief, they found her in good health and well cared for by her husband, the Reindeer. The children were healthier than their cousins, and their clothing was clean and well made. The Reindeer, in the meantime, was grazing in the tundra and would not return for at least another month. The parents, pleased with the conditions in which their daughter was living, decided to stay for a longer visit. Their daughter welcomed them and said that her husband insisted on a clean household. She asked her parents to help her do her work because Reindeer did not like to see idleness.

When he returned home, Reindeer jumped across the threshold of the house and turned into a man. He was pleased to see his wife's parents, and for some time they lived happily together. The Reindeer/man had always explained to his wife that she should keep their sleeping robes clean and throw away old hides. However, one day, while his wife was going through old items, she thought she could dry some older hides in the sun, and there would be no need to throw them away. When the Reindeer/man returned home from the tundra, he was struck by the smell of rotting skin. He turned back into a reindeer and trotted off into the tundra. The children, including an infant in a cradle, also turned into reindeer, and joined their father in the tundra.

The myth ends with a warning to the listeners, admonishing against idleness and dirtiness and encouraging work and cleanliness.

A STRUCTURAL ANALYSIS OF THE STORY OF MYANDASH

While the Myandash myth is worthy of appreciation as a beautiful story, it can also be analyzed to determine deeper levels of meaning. Because it is the origin myth of the Russian Sami, it deserves full exploration to uncover its essential truths. The following structural analysis of the Myandash myth applies

---

[1] A second version of this story explains that the children were completely human.

[2] Cabins, dotted across the tundra, are used as homes by the reindeer herders.

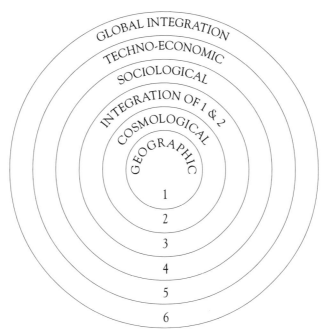

GLOBAL INTEGRATION
TECHNO-ECONOMIC
SOCIOLOGICAL
INTEGRATION OF 1 & 2
COSMOLOGICAL
GEOGRAPHIC

1

2

3

4

5

6

LAYERS OF MYTH ANALYSIS

the methodology of Claude Lévi-Strauss, professor at the Collège de France and continental Europe's most distinguished living anthropologist (Lévi-Strauss, 1955; Leach, 1967:vii). Professor Lévi-Strauss argues that all myths contain two aspects: sequences and schemata. The sequences are the obvious, apparent content of the myth: the characters, what they do, in what chronological order, etc. (Leach, 1967:17-21). The schemata are clusters of information organized on different planes or levels of abstraction. While the sequences are linear, the schemata are vertically integrated throughout the myth, and they may interact with one another in subtle ways. In *The Story of Asdiwal* (Leach, 1967:1-47), Lévi-Strauss describes how six individual schemata—geographic, cosmological, integration, sociological, techno-economic, and global integration—intertwine to form one schema. We can use the same six schemata to begin to unravel the story of Myandash, or Reindeer/man.

To begin with, the Myandash myth follows a linear path of sequences. Parents produce three daughters, who in due time take three husbands. The parents dutifully go to visit each daughter after their marriages are established

North Salma tundra.

and discover an odd and hurtful set of individual circumstances. Only one marriage shows promise, but it too involves struggle for the favoured daughter. Just what is the Myandash myth telling the Sami at its more complex levels? Let us now return to Lévi-Strauss's six interlocked schemata.

At the geographic level of structural analysis, the Myandash myth tells us about three possible locales of marriage in the Kola Peninsula: the sea, the air, and the land. Seal's marriage den is in the ocean; Raven's is a nest in the sky world; Myandash's is on the tundra. When the world was new, the Sami were exploring their possible homelands: three options were apparent, and choices had to be made.

At the cosmological level of analysis, the origin myth suggests that the three daughters had what can now be viewed as special powers. Seal's wife could live in the ocean; Raven's wife was at home in a nest; and Myandash's wife was at home on the tundra, far from her parents. While the Sami today are still at home on the tundra, none can live at sea or in the air. And what Sami women would continue to live today with arm-eating or eye-pecking husbands? Furthermore, no Sami children today are half-seal, half-raven, or half-reindeer. Today, all Sami have human form, but they are closest to the

Another view of North Salma tundra.

reindeer in spirit, in mind, and perhaps—because they love to eat reindeer meat—in body. Indeed, the most spiritually pure Sami existence is living out on the tundra with the reindeer. That is why the old Sami today say that if the reindeer all disappear, there can be no Sami culture, and no Sami.

The integration of the geographic and the cosmological schemata reveals the whys of Sami land selection and mate selection for all to hear and follow. It is the natural order of things for Sami women to live with the reindeer on the tundra and to marry herders so that, like the wife of Myandash, they must also lose their children to the herding life. Just as Myandash's human-form children run across the threshold after their father and become reindeer, so will all Sami children "become like Reindeer" in their natural quest for adulthood.

At the sociological level of analysis, the Myandash myth reveals the nuclear family and neolocal aspects of Sami social organization. The original family unit in the story consists of mother, father, and three daughters. The daughters all must move away and establish neolocal residence with their husbands. None of the three new households also contains the husband's parents. It is clear, however, that a wife's parents will come to visit, and the purpose of the visit is to determine just how happy their daughter is with her husband. From the visit, one could infer a potential return to the parents' home if the husband is maltreating his wife and children.

At the techno-economic level of analysis, the Myandash story reveals a variety of details. Seals make their homes out of the bones of animals; ravens live in nests of twigs; and Reindeer/man lives in a cabin. Furthermore, Myandash likes his home to be clean, and instructs his wife to take care of the reindeer skins and keep them clean. He also does not mind that old skins should be thrown away. The key is to keep the tundra home clean, free from decay and foul smells, and generally hygienic for the children. Myandash is so revolted by the bad housekeeping of his wife that he runs away, assumes reindeer form, and takes the children with him. Could there be a more obvious message?

The final schema is a global integration, and it involves assessing the origin myth for initial and final states of affairs. It may also involve determining which schema carries the strongest message. In essence, the global integration function is mediation of cultural conflict. The purpose of the origin myth is to inform its Sami listeners of contradictions in life, and to explain them away (Leach, 1967:99-100). The Myandash myth starts with neolocal experimentation. Two of the daughters have definitely chosen the wrong mates. The world of the sea and the world of the air are not the chosen Sami domain. The tundra is the best place to live, and Myandash is the best husband.

The parents decide to stay with Myandash and his family. This form of residence (neolocal with maternal extended family present) represents the ultimate, best-case scenario in the myth.

At the core of the myth is an interesting message: even the best daughter and best wife may not be as good as Reindeer/man. Myandash leaves her, taking along his now fully reindeer children, because of her misguided housekeeping practices. Clearly Reindeer/man knows best. So when conflict arises between reindeer and the Sami, the reindeer's desires should be closely heeded. The meaning of the Myandash myth is simply this: *what is good for the reindeer is good for the Sami.* And it may be assumed that this core of meaning has application across all of the schemata that operate in the myth. It is a statement of the very essence of Sami life in the tundra lands of the Kola Peninsula.

John Andreas Savio, To the Mountains, *woodcut, 22cm x 17cm*

Eighteenth-century Sami Siida meeting (Leems, 1767).

CHAPTER 4
THE PRACTICE OF CO-MANAGEMENT IN CANADA AND ITS RELEVANCE FOR RUSSIA

The concept of co-management has had just over a decade of legislated application in northern Canada, through the Inuvialuit (1984), Gwich'in (1992), Sahtu (1994), and Nunavut (1995) comprehensive land-claim settlements, negotiated with the federal government and now entrenched in the Canadian Constitution Act (1982). Reduced to basics, and using the Inuvialuit settlement in the western Arctic as an example, co-management involves combining indigenous and cultural environmental wisdom about wildlife (fish, birds, ungulates, whales, etc.) with scientific knowledge in the cause of taking management decisions about proposed government, industrial, or community development that may affect land, water, wildlife, and (ultimately) people. It is a joint management process that brings local resource users and government representatives together to share the responsibility for managing local or regional resources and monitoring the effects of development on the population (Roberts, 1994:1). This process involves placing holders of traditional and cultural environmental wisdom in the same room with environmental scientists, and then convening a meeting to hear submissions by project proponents about potential impacts. Possessed of the facts, and aware of the local and regional issues, the co-management committee then analyzes situations and takes decisions which influence and may bind the proponents in the conduct of their proposed work. In rendering their decisions, co-management committees, such as the Inuvialuit Environmental Impact Screening Committee (EISC) or the higher-order decision maker called the Environmental Impact Review Board (EIRB), also require skilled facilitators to act as chairpersons. Decisions are rendered by consensus in the vast majority of cases, although the provision for a tie-breaking vote from the chair always exists. In this way, the Inuvialuit EISC, based in Inuvik, Northwest Territories, currently processes over 50 project proposals for development on Inuvialuit or shared government/Inuvialuit lands each year. The committee can screen any proposal pursuant to any regulatory process in the Inuvialuit settlement area; refer a proposal back to the drawing board for more information or detail; or refer contentious, larger projects for full-scale

Nina Afanas'eva introduces the project partners in Lovozero, May 1995.

environmental review by the EIRB. The range of applications considered by
the EISC includes projects as diverse as establishing gravel pits, expanding
airport runways, creating family-owned tourist ventures, and exploring for
huge volumes of natural gas and oil beneath the fixed ice of the Beaufort Sea.
When the committee is in session, the EISC waiting room can hold southern
Canadian business people, regional entrepreneurs, and foreign venture
capitalists spending their first day in the North.

There was no co-management regime in the Inuvialuit settlement region
before the settlement of the comprehensive land claim in 1984. Previously,
the federal government, with the minor and largely administrative assistance
of the Government of the Northwest Territories, had adjudicated development
issues "in the best interests" of local residents, with only token input from the
residents themselves. This system resulted in the late 1960s and early 1970s
in approvals for oil and gas exploration activities without any local awareness,
consultation, or input (Usher and Noble, 1975). Needless to say, local hunters
and trappers felt that they had no say in the development of their homelands,
and feared the worst from an industry and a technology about which they
knew little. Political organization followed, greatly influenced by the rapid
increase in oil and gas drilling permits in the Beaufort region, and finally by
the proposal for a large-diameter pipeline to transport natural gas from Inuvik
down the Mackenzie Valley to Alberta, the gateway to southern Canadian
and American energy markets. The Inuvialuit comprehensive claim settlement
is one tangible outcome of this era of northern development; ironically, large-

The co-management project is defined by the Sami, May 1995.

scale natural gas and oil production from the western Arctic is still unachieved.

Today in southern Canada, the study and promotion of co-management have come to support the careers of a growing number of academics, consultants, and government and industry employees. The Canadian literature on co-management continues to grow dramatically, and all of this is happening in a late-1990s economic climate that pits the bush economy against the industrial economy, and conservationists against developers. It should also be noted that, except for the comprehensive claims of the James Bay Cree (1978) in Quebec and the Nisga'a in British Columbia (Nisga'a Treaty Negotiations, 1996), Canada has no legislated basis for co-management south of 60°N latitude. Consequently, a debate has begun in provincial and industrial circles about the efficacy of the term *management* in the concept of co-management. Co-management implies the right to participate and the practice of directive rather than advisory authority. Rights flow from legislation, and— apart from the two examples cited above—southern Canada has no provincial or federal legislation to permit the exercise of co-management by First Nations on Treaty or provincial Crown lands. However, co-management is being practised by agreement in several provinces: for instance, in the Queen Charlotte Islands off British Columbia's northwest coast, the Haida Indians and the federal agency Parks Canada, in accordance with the Gwaii Haanas Agreement (1984), have created an Archipelago Management Board to oversee cooperatively all actions related to the planning, operation, and management of the Gwaii Haanas National Park Reserve.

In practice, this means that Haida and Parks Canada representatives sit on a committee that controls the park development process in Gwaii Haanas for the benefit of all Canadians. The Archipelago Management Board regulates total tourist nights per year (14,000 in 1997), allocates tourist business licences to local and outside entrepreneurs, and specifies how interpretation services will be provided at designated Haida cultural sites. The current budget for operating all of the co-management services in the Gwaii Haanas National Park Reserve is $2.5 million.

While the intellectual climate for co-management in the south has blossomed, those who would seek its application on provincial Crown and First Nations Treaty lands are currently faced with strong opposition. Opponents cite the lack of legislated authority, but they also lack the willingness to share management of provincially authorized resource allocations, such as forest management agreements and tree farm licences, that permit large companies to harvest forest resources on Crown lands. Recently, some progress has been made in the fishing industry in British Columbia, where job losses and the threat of species extinction have compelled the various sectors to create new, cooperative round tables to allocate resources in the region (Glavin, 1996). Berkes (1985:205-206) also reports the success of co-management or even management regime development when previous systems of no-management threaten the death of the resource. According to his analysis of the living resources management "life cycle," governments are never more happy to pass authority and responsibility to First Nations (especially) than when all the trees have already been clear-cut, or all the fish have been caught at the end of the "sequential exploitation" phase of the cycle. Clearly, the time to develop practical co-management regimes is when there are still significant wildlife populations to manage.

One cannot assume that all of the impediments to creating new co-management regimes for healthy ecosystems stem from purely legalistic grounds. Also at play (and sometimes masked by the legal arguments) are racist agendas that hold that First Nations people "are not scientists," that they are illiterate, that they work only with anecdotal evidence, and that they are now "too removed from the land" to properly manage wildlife populations any more.

The above arguments proceed from superficial observation and rely on superficial analysis to reach superficial conclusions. Indeed, Ph.Ds in science are not yet widely held by members of First Nations communities; many elders rich in traditional knowledge and wisdom do not read English or even an orthography of their language; the bush economy does rely on memory reinforced by anecdote to pass on knowledge to younger generations; and many new First Nations communities have been (and are still being) created more for the administrative convenience of government than for the benefit of cultural tradition in the bush. To infer from these observations that the bush economy is dead, or that its promise is fading, is to deny current and future opportunities to people and cultures who have evolved in a symbiotic relationship with the land and biota in the ecosystem. To infer that this relationship is flawed or passé is to miss the point that it reflects almost the entire history of man's relationship with nature on this planet. For over fifteen thousand years, *homo sapiens* and our predecessors have lived as extended families of hunter-gatherers in deserts, forests, and tundra. During this time much has been learned, internalized, and orally transmitted to each successive generation. As a result of this means of learning, women and men became culturally embedded in the practice of empiricism. We literally are who we are on the basis of experience; our knowledge is rooted in trial and error; and for most of our existence on earth we have talked—not written—about our collective wisdom.

When examined in this context, racism directed against the surviving members of land-based economies can be seen to be a form of denial. It emanates from the experience of only the last 15,000 years—the period that has seen agricultural economies take root and produce the seeds of industrialism and corporatism, specialization, written language, and the university-promoted cult of professional expertise. Against the empiricism of four million years, we now seek to oppose the relatively infantile experience of the last 15,000. Somehow, in the practice of sedentary agriculture and the production of annual crop surpluses to tide us all over the winters, we have come to assume that our prior experience is irrelevant. How ironic that we steadfastly hold this course in the face of global warming, monstrous human population increases, expedited species extinction, and rapid natural resource depletion. Surely it should be obvious to most that prior to our global infatuation with agriculture, we experienced great stability as an evolving species, did not fundamentally challenge natural processes in our home ecosystems, and carefully worked to preserve relationships of balance with the natural world. Before agriculture, we did not conceive of dominion; rather, we worked to the ideal of survival on the land. While this survival is now mocked as evidence of individual lives that were solitary, brutish, and short, we cannot lose sight of the fact that in those lives our collective footprint on the earth was appropriate to our evolutionary needs and to those of our non-human neighbours. Recapturing just some of that human spirit and experience is the objective of co-management.

TRADITIONAL (AND CULTURAL) LAND-USE AND OCCUPANCY MAPPING

Effective co-management practice requires that traditional environmental wisdom and contemporary popular knowledge of the bush economy be mapped. This concept is clearly Canadian in its theoretical development and application. The first traditional land-use mapping studies, undertaken as part of the preparation for comprehensive land-claim settlements in the North, focused on Inuit knowledge of the littoral zone of the eastern High Arctic (Freeman Research Ltd., 1976). Subsequent studies moved the methodology to Labrador (Brice-Bennett, 1977) and to northeastern British Columbia (Brody, 1981), where the study purposes began to reflect the need to forecast megaproject impact on bush economy community, lifestyle, and subsistence issues. In this respect, British author Hugh Brody began to move land-use mapping from the academic to the political realm in Canada, even to the point of personally testifying on aboriginal land-use issues before regulatory hearings. While Brody's 1981 book, *Maps and Dreams*, had a definite role to play in enabling the Treaty 8 residents of northeastern British Columbia to demonstrate their Treaty rights to hunting, fishing, and gathering, it was more squarely aimed at illustrating how traditional environmental wisdom and aboriginal wildlife management systems have to be considered in major linear developments like natural gas pipelines. Since *Maps and Dreams*, the focus of traditional land-use and occupancy mapping projects has moved to smaller oil and gas projects in the provincial mid-North, and to forestry megaprojects in the Canadian boreal forest. Inevitably, the academic focus has continued to merge with political objectives.

Today in northern British Columbia and Alberta, a variety of such projects have been recently started or completed by the Arctic Institute, the First Nations and Metis communities, and a variety of government and corporate sponsors. Together, these myriad organizations and communities have entered into joint funding agreements to create atlases and geographic information systems (GIS) based on participatory research methodology, which trains local people in their home communities to undertake their own research. Implicit in all of this research is the gathering of traditional and current cultural information about aboriginal wildlife management and the seasonal round of scheduling and procurement that is at the heart of the bush economy. The resulting map products therefore combine harvest sites for fish, birds, fur-bearing animals, ungulates, berries, trees, and medicinal plants, and the fixed sites of cabins, associated trails, graves, and historic areas. When researchers overlay these data sets upon each other (either manually or with the aid of GIS), they can create a snapshot of bush life and land use that is comprehensive, inherently visual rather than literary, and inclusive of many peoples' popular knowledge and wisdom. Such maps permit us, usually for the first time, to compare external industrial-economy development proposals with current (and past) land use in the bush economy. This visual comparison is typically the first step in assessing trade-offs, forming community partnerships for conservation and business development, and moving to cooperative rather than confrontational modes of interaction in the development cycle.

METHODOLOGY FOR MAPPING

The basic methodology for traditional land-use and occupancy studies has been described in *Mapping How We Use Our Land* (Robinson et al., 1994). Key to the methodology is a participatory approach that involves training local people to conduct interviews that meet basic social science standards for qualitative and exploratory research with elders and other current bush economy participants. Participatory action research (PAR) projects typically originate from a known community need and a strong community desire to manage the process from start to finish. A community advisory committee (or CAC), and a technical advisory committee (or TAC) are generally organized to provide direction, support, and assistance to the projects. An outside non-governmental organization, such as a research institute, is typically involved in providing the PAR research training and ensuring that the methodological means are present to achieve the desired community ends. PAR is best suited to communities that desire intensive community involvement and seek lasting change in lives, circumstances, and economic and power relationships.

The purpose of the interviews in land-use and occupancy studies is to get bush users to define the areas of their use, the species harvested, and the infrastructure necessary to live in the bush. The Arctic Institute's methodology now involves up to 200 species and fixed-site icons (cabins, trails, fish camps, cemeteries, etc.), which users place individually on maps during the interview process. Species icons are placed on harvest locations; fixed-site icons go on their actual or remembered locations. Interviews are guided by a protocol (not a questionnaire) that suggests questions for the respondents to think about and potentially answer. Generally, interviews are conducted in the language of the respondent's choice, and most interviews are conducted individually. Group interviews are occasionally conducted when requested or obviously called for in the process. An example of such need is elders' collective desire to meet together to refresh their memories about life in an old bush community that now may be abandoned.

Collective meetings are scheduled to provide peer validation of either work in progress or completed projects. Such validation meetings basically gather all respondents together for tea and fried bread and a review of map displays. Participants are encouraged to review all data sets and report errors or omissions. Discussions are convened around contentious issues, and consensus is sought for all changes and corrections. Experience has shown that this validation process works equally well in First Nations communities in the provincial mid-North and north of 60° in Canada.

Another form of validation is enabled by the use of global positioning technology (GPS). This validation occurs when a community trainee takes a hand-held GPS computer into the bush and records the precise positions of sites with the push of a button. Using United States military satellites in fixed orbits overhead as reference, the GPS captures exact latitude and longitude coordinates in electronic files, which are later downloaded into the GIS for storage, data manipulation, and mapping.

Once the working maps (generally at both 1:50,000 and 1:200,000 scale) are complete, they are ready for desktop system conversion to atlas format, or GPS validation and GIS printing. At this time, the Arctic Institute is still experimenting with both approaches, and with different allied software systems. Our icon-mapping approach does not require GPS validation of sites in the bush, produces clear maps at the scale of choice, and allows expeditious production of publications. The downside of this approach, however, is that precise locations are unavailable, and re-location of sites in the bush is dependent on local knowledge developed and held by the PAR trainees over the course of their training.

The use of GIS and GPS as means of mapping and validation raises important issues related to the appropriateness of the technology itself. We knew that within the context of the Kola Sami in Russia, a GPS instrument linked to American satellites would clearly be highly inappropriate. In one of the most militarized zones in the world, use of this equipment might put the community in danger and would certainly make our work in Russia difficult, if not impossible.

However, aside from the potential allegation of espionage, the use of this technology raises a much more fundamental question of appropriateness. How much more effective is this technique for land-use mapping than the cost-effective methods being applied now? Can small indigenous communities in Canada or Russia spare the funds to buy such equipment? What capacity does the community have in terms of trained personnel to effectively use the GIS containing their traditional knowledge? To what extent does reliance upon GIS technology create dependence on purchase of more and more technology in the spirit of keeping up with the latest program? At what point does reliance on GIS cease to be an effective tool and become a burdensome financial and human capital investment? To what degree does the use of GIS, now widespread among corporations, mitigate a community's control of its own knowledge? In a co-management structure, this knowledge could be electronically transmitted across the globe with ease. These are important considerations for indigenous communities in Russia or Canada. They are also important for non-governmental academic institutions such as ours. On the Sami Co-Management Project, for example, community members expressed deep concern that the information being mapped be carefully protected. If certain information were made available to poachers or tourism firms, it would seriously compromise the livelihood and safety of the reindeer herders. The maps in this book were approved for release by the Kola Sami Association and reflect the Sami desire for global awareness of their precarious situation.

Another linked methodological concern is the question of paradigms. Traditional knowledge emerges from a context, carrying with it the cultural and spiritual values of its people. It is at once universal and specific. By definition, anything "traditional" is based on the sacredness of time and custom. Mapping this knowledge by hand or by GIS gives us only a small window into the cosmology from which it emerges. Does a Cartesian rendering of traditional knowledge in a map format empty this knowledge of its cultural and spiritual context? Are we engaging in a utilitarian exercise that perceives traditional knowledge as yet another instrument for maintaining the market system? This question becomes doubly significant in Russia, because we are working not only with an indigenous community, but within an environment where the Soviet experiment failed after 70 years and the market system is pressing itself on the populace. This context raises additional anxieties related to appropriateness.

Ultimately the responses to these questions can come only from the indigenous communities themselves. Nonetheless, it is our role as a partner of the community and as an academic institution to reflect on the appropriateness of the methods applied to mapping traditional knowledge.

Raphael Kaplinsky (1990) determines appropriateness on the basis of the following four components:
- technical efficiency (not being wasteful)
- economic efficiency (using locally available materials)
- environmental compatibility
- social and cultural compatibility.

These criteria suggest that appropriateness is context-specific. What is appropriate in one indigenous community may not be appropriate to another.

BENEFITTING FROM RECENT SCANDINAVIAN RESEARCH
The Scandinavian Sami, who are the Russian Sami's closest neighbours, have been subjected to scientific research for a long time (Bäck, 1996:183-211). Only over the last few decades has this research begun to focus on social and

John Andreas Savio, Confrontation 1, *woodcut, 19.5cm x 26.5cm*

economic issues, and to include the contributions of anthropologists, ethnologists, archaeologists, lawyers, historians, and linguists (Lasko, 1994). Government-authorized research, sponsored by the Swedish Council for Forestry and Agricultural Research, began in 1990 to focus on the Swedish reindeer industry (Bäck, 1996), and in particular on understanding natural resource conflicts in the Swedish reindeer herding areas. Perhaps predictably, the forest industry is today exerting the greatest pressures on Sami reindeer pastures, and Swedish academics from the Department of Social and Economic Geography of Uppsala University are studying forest/pasture conflicts in Sweden's northernmost province. Rather than employ participatory action methodologies, they have chosen to focus on GIS applications to analyze spatial variation and land use, and on archival materials relating to Swedish Sami history over the last one hundred years. Interestingly, industrial developments and associated access roads have made the greatest impacts on the reindeer herd migrations in Sweden. The development of hydroelectric power, in particular, has flooded or decreased access to pasture lands, to the point that approximately one percent of net pasture lands have been lost. About one-third of these lands are critical winter pasture land (Vattenkraften och rennäringen, 1986:10).

While industrial threats to pasture lands remain, Swedish Sami now worry about other potential threats to reindeer posed by tourism. They especially "fear over-exploitation of the mountain region for the purpose of short-run economic gains by outside interests involved in tourism" (Bäck, 1996:196). While there may also be opportunities for Sami tourism to develop, there is a desire that it be of appropriate scale and environmentally benign.

While the military is not an immediate threat to the Swedish Sami, certain facilities expose individual villages to localized threats. Bäck notes that "the predominating opinion among the informants is that the military represents an asset, because of the help it provides in preparing migration routes" (Bäck, 1996:200). While the Swedish Sami face specific problems similar to those facing the Russian Sami, we shall see that the degree of their input to research and policy mitigation is quite different in scale and substance.

Johan Klemet Kalstad, a Sami academic author from Norway writing in *Sami Culture in a New Era* (1997), has recently suggested that co-management could be useful for managing Sami lands collectively. Drawing on the Canadian literature, and specifically the Inuvialuit Final Agreement of 1984, Kalstad comments on the special knowledge of local user groups and its potential contribution to "a more comprehensive decision making accorded developing communities where the traditional economy based on land and animals is the core..." (1997:121). He calls for the Sami Parliament to initiate the process of co-operation, and for the design of efficient structures and bodies to maintain land use which acknowledges Sami "rights, power and obligations with respect to management of resources in a particular area" (1997:123). Kalstad's desire for action is just as relevant in Russia as it is in Scandinavia.

RELEVANCE FOR THE SAMI AND FOR RUSSIA

When the Kola Sami Co-Management Project was conceptualized by Lloyd Binder, Nina Afanas'eva, Tat'yana Louk'yanchenko, and Mike Robinson in 1994, we knew that the concept had yet to be introduced to Russia. This alone gave us energy for the task. We also knew that the need of the Sami was great because of the recent Ponoy River lease agreement between the Murmansk Oblast and Lovozero municipal authorities and American and Finnish entrepreneurs. This 15-year lease has rendered the largest river in the Kola region, the Ponoy, off limits to resident Sami salmon fishers, and resulted in the immediate loss of between 40 and 80 tonnes of salmon protein per season to the collective Sami diet (Nina Afanas'eva, pers. comm.) In an attempt to counteract the impacts of this lease agreement, the Sami started small tourism, fishing, and reindeer-breeding enterprises. However, these small businesses have proven uncompetitive with the large operators. A Sami tourist campground on a river that the Sami currently own was recently burnt down. Two reindeer breeding companies have also been formed, but since the federal Russian Land Act has not been ratified, the companies could obtain only 25-year leases to their pasture land. For the first five years of the leases, the land use is free; thereafter, high rent must be paid (Roberts et al., 1996:16-17). A new gold mine, a natural gas pipeline from offshore in the Barents Sea, and several forestry projects are also in the offing for the Kola Peninsula, and further road-building projects are known to be contemplated. All of this projected development will also entail the construction of new access roads, increased helicopter overflights of the tundra, and increased community tensions in Lovozero and Jona. Meanwhile some 60,000 head of reindeer still undertake their annual migrations from forest to coast and back across the Kola tundra. As we demonstrated in the Myandash myth analysis, *what is good for the reindeer is good for the Sami.* Conversely, what is bad for the reindeer is bad for the Sami. Tat'yana Louk'yanchenko (pers. comm.) put it this way: "If there are no reindeer, there can be no Sami culture."

As a consequence of the above, the partners realized that it was time to conceptualize, propose, and actively lobby for the introduction of a co-management regime in the Kola Peninsula. The project began this task with some significant obstacles:

- The Kola Sami Association, the political constituent assembly of the Sami, is not considered an official organization by the Murmansk Duma and its committees.
- The Sami are represented by a small Oblast bureaucracy, the Committee on Northern Peoples, but the Sami do not themselves feel any loyalty to this committee. There is no legal recognition of the Sami homeland on the tundra.

When contemplating these problems during an interview in Lovozero in July 1996, senior brigade herder Nikolai Lukin commented:

> I do not think I will get the chance to see the fruits of such co-management. The Sami have some special rights which the Russians, the Komi, and the Nenets don't have. Now it happens that poachers come to our camps and say, "We have already been here for eight years shooting animals, so please leave this place." I say to them, "You are occupying our land." On the border between my brigade and the neighbouring brigade, there are obviously very rich minerals to be found. If they dig these minerals, I doubt they will ask us for permission.

In spite of this general pessimism about the prospects for establishing co-management in Russia, Mr. Lukin concluded his interview by saying: "If you don't do anything, nothing will happen!" Clearly it is time to act.

CHAPTER 5
FIRST STEPS FOR MAPPING THE PATTERN OF SAMI LAND USE

In determining the methodology for the Sami Co-Management Project, the project partners had to consider the cultural reality of the Kola. The PAR process found favour with the Sami, who liked the idea of learning how to map their land using the process developed by the Arctic Institute for its Canadian projects. Consequently, a three-week travelling/training workshop was held in November 1995 in Canada, involving work in Calgary and Wabasca/Desmarais, Alberta, and Inuvik, Northwest Territories. During this time Nina Afanas'eva, the Sami Association president, her colleagues Larisa Avdeeva and Tat'yana Tsmykailo, the presidents of the Sami Associations of Lovozero and Jona, and Dr. Tat'yana Louk'yanchenko, of the Moscow-based Institute of Ethnology and Anthropology, participated in methodology seminars, visited Canadian mapping projects, and attended an international conference on co-management organized by the Arctic Institute and the Inuvialuit Game Council in Inuvik.

Out of this preparatory period evolved a set of specially designed Sami mapping icons, agreement on Lovozero and Jona base maps (at 1:200,000 scale), and a detailed Russian-language interview protocol for use in the Lovozero and Jona interviews. The Arctic Institute partners next agreed to produce the maps and icons in Calgary, and the Sami agreed to begin the interview process in earnest in the early spring of 1996.

Also present at the Canadian training workshop was Galina Andreeva, chairperson of the Murmansk Duma's committee for science, education, culture, and nationalities. Ms. Andreeva's presence was very important, both to help us understand how the Kola Peninsula regulatory systems worked and to introduce her to Canadian counterparts in northern Alberta and Inuvik. She was also instrumental in explaining that GPS technology would not be permitted in Russia for reasons of state security. Thus informed, we jointly determined to map only with icons on the 1:200,000 scale working maps. To ensure the best quality for the final product, the Arctic Institute would prepare two plastic-encased, four-colour base maps for the Kola Peninsula, showing the areas around Jona and Lovozero, using several map sheets purchased in Murmansk.

After the Canadian workshop, both Russians and Canadians went to work on their respective assignments. In Lovozero and Jona, more than 80 interviews were conducted; English language lessons were arranged for the eight mapping trainees; and apartments were painted, wallpapered, and scrubbed for the Canadian members of the team to use in July 1996. In Canada, customized Russian Sami icons were drawn and mass-produced on plastic film with adhesive backing; the base maps were sealed in protective plastic coverings; and the protocol document was translated into Russian. Weekly faxes, coordinated by project translator Leif Rantala in Rovaniemi, Finland, kept all parties up to date on our progress.

As the days and weeks flew by in the spring of 1996, the political situation in Russia began to cause the Arctic Institute's board members some concern. The presidential election was looming, and statements by Messrs. Yeltsin, Lebed, and Zhirinovskii to the Western press suggested that, should Mr. Yeltsin lose the presidency, the transition of power would be anything but peaceful. Still naive about Russian politics, and harbouring fears that we had learned in the Cold War days, the Canadian partners began to strategize "Plan B." Why not conduct our mapping work in Finland? We asked Leif Rantala if the University of Lapland in Rovaniemi might have appropriate space that we could rent for the work and accommodation. We contacted the new Canadian Ambassador to Russia, Anne Leahey, for advice. The Embassy duly reported that it had checked with a Dr. Tat'yana Louk'yanchenko at the Moscow-based Institute of Ethnology and Anthropology, and had been assured that all would be safe for our work in Murmansk and the Kola villages. Tat'yana Louk'yanchenko next faxed the Canadians asking politely why we had not contacted her, our partner, directly with these concerns! Next, news arrived from Leif Rantala that Larisa Avdeeva was most upset about moving the work to Finland: she feared that the Canadians were becoming like a recent group of Scandinavians, who had promised much, but left before completing their program as described. Meanwhile, the news of Russia in the Calgary newspapers became more and more upsetting. At the April meeting of the Arctic Institute's national board in Ottawa, the Canadian concerns were debated and weighed. After two hours of discussion, the mapping team were told to rely on their own sense of the mission's safety, and to go only if they felt it would be safe. Two months later, we left for Russia. Ringing in our ears was Larisa Avdeeva's lament, "Why is it the farther you get from Mother Russia, the more afraid of us you become?"

The air flight via Heathrow to Kiruna, northern Sweden, went smoothly. We travelled to Mertejarvi, where we rented a ten-year-old Saab 900 from Helge Utsi, Lloyd Binder's uncle, and began our trip overland to Murmansk via the Ivalo, Finland border crossing. Back home in Calgary, family and friends had requested sequential phone calls en route to confirm our whereabouts and safety. A last call was placed at the Petsamo Motel in Ivalo before we entered Russia on July 8, accompanied by our translator Leif Rantala. The trip to Murmansk was largely uneventful. Unlike the year before, the border guards did not point the way to the customs buildings with their rifles, they did not search our vehicles, and the sandy road surface had recently been topped with gravel: Murmansk seemed as inviting as an old friend.

On July 9, we drove to Lovozero, arriving in the late afternoon to meet our partners and comrades. We were shown to our apartments, which had been selected for their prominent views of the village, and immediately invited to a celebratory dinner that evening. A higher standard of welcome could not have been offered in Calgary, and we were gently mocked for our Western fears of Russian politics.

ON WITH THE MAPPING

Armed with our methodology, our newly minted maps and icons, the extensive body of detail gleaned from the village interviews, and the enthusiasm of the Lovozero mapping trainees (Pavel Fefelov, Nadya Zolotuhina, and Andrei Gavrilov, headed by Larisa Avdeeva), we got to work on July 10. Elder Andrei Gavrilov placed that first reindeer icon on the map, as Canadian and Sami partners watched with joy and expectation.

The children welcome us to Jona, May 1995.

CHAPTER 6:
A WALK THROUGH JONA, JULY 1996

Today I am a resident of Jona, a small village in the Kola Peninsula. Established ca. 1870 by Finns to take advantage of good fishing and hunting in the region, it now has about 300 inhabitants, of whom about 80 are Sami. Their families were forced by federal government decree to settle in Jona in 1936-37, as Stalin sought to collectivize the Sami and their reindeer in communal farms. Prior to Stalin's initiatives, herding families of the Babino Sami (their traditional name, from their former village of Babinsk) had ranged free with their reindeer in the lake and forest region to the north and west. Under the new Communist system, those who refused to give up family reindeer ownership were classed as *kulaks* (agricultural capitalists, and therefore enemies of the state), and their animals and fishing nets were confiscated. Those herders who refused to be collectivized were arrested and sent away to *gulags*, most never to be seen again. Some men were shot in the new village as a lesson to other dissenters. Meanwhile, large areas of their traditional herding and pasture lands were enclosed in the Lappish National Park, established in the early 1930s and placed out of bounds to all but scientific parties and officials.

Drying sigs on a clothesline in Jona.

Perestroika chicken coops and piggeries in Jona.

Butchering the pig.

Reduced to meagre rations and collective farming, the Jona Sami next had to survive a global depression and World War II, which saw Jona, only 80 kilometres from the Finnish frontier, become a vast recuperation community for Russian partisans making attacks into Finland. In the 1950s, a mine was established at the nearby town of Kovdor, and Russian southerners were recruited to run it. Sami labour was bypassed when Russians needed jobs. In 1972, a state farm called Sovkhoz Jonskii, which included a dairy with 800 cows, was established in Jona. Its managers were all southerners, and they changed every second year. The dairy was meant to replace the collective reindeer herding farm, which was failing because of poaching, disinterest, wolves, and disease. By the early 1980s the dairy was in trouble, and the Sami had to turn to survival fishing and potato gardens for food. The advent of *perestroika* in 1985 resulted in the near-total collapse of the state farm[3], as management and workers sold the cows for cash to buy cars and food. In a last-ditch attempt to preserve the dairy business, the farm was privatized and assumed a new form as a joint stock company. While this form of corporate organization may harken back to Sami traditions of private reindeer ownership and management from the pre-Stalin era, very few present-day Jona Sami can explain how it works or who owns the shares. Although a large, prefabricated concrete fence has been erected around the state farm's perimeter, it has not prevented the theft of feed, livestock, and equipment. The current manager, a Moldavian, is ridiculed for having built "the Great Wall of Moldavia" around the state farm at the same time that the Berlin wall was being taken down. Inside, perhaps 150 cows remain.

Alya and Yuliya, members of the Jona Sami mapping team, are both eager to walk around their village to show me how things have changed since my last visit in May 1995. Alya is Yuliya's aunt, and together they have benefitted from growing up Sami in Jona. Their experience of the impact of *perestroika* is rooted in village life, as seen through the eyes of a parent, in Alya's case, and those of a second-year university student, in Yuliya's case. After a 10-hour work day with the maps and a feast-like dinner of mashed Jona *kartoshka* (potatoes), *sig* (a small whitefish), *ogurtsy* (cucumbers) from the Murmansk

---

[3]   By July 1997, the vocational school of Lovozero, No. 26, had taken over the former state farm.

44

greenhouses, thinly sliced sausage, and penne, we set out for an evening stroll. The July sun is still high in the sky as we walk up to the *Dom Kultury* (House of Culture), which is now closed. "No more money for culture! What do you think of that?" asks Yuliya. Next we cross over the paved two-lane Kovdor highway to visit the meteorological station. It too is closed. "Again—no more money," says Alya. By now the newly hatched mosquitoes are swarming over my head and reaching far into my shirt sleeves and pants. We walk about the neglected rain gauges, thermometers, wind vanes, and barometers, and notice how much of the surrounding soil is now cultivated for potatoes. We next cross back over the Kovdor road and head north on the main village street. Just ahead is the inevitable three-storey, prefabricated, Russian general-issue apartment block. This one is almost entirely vacant. A group of young adolescent boys peer and jeer at us from a second-storey flat, all of whose windows are broken. "They go there to drink vodka," says Alya. At the last communal stairway in this apartment, Yuliya tells us: "This was the library. What do you think of that?" We climb the smelly, dark stairs to the second floor and enter the old library space. It is all strewn with broken glass, and no books are left on any of the shelves. Every window has been smashed. We leave almost immediately. "Watch out—it is dangerous!" calls Yuliya, who has gone ahead of me down the stairs. Outside again we go by the Jona *reka* (river), towards the west, the now setting sun, and the community gardens. To our left is the community *magazin* (store). It is padlocked shut, and we look through the window at a small pile of Murmansk *ogurtsy*, some litre containers of milk, and darkness. On we go to complete our circle tour. Ahead are some new buildings, all made of scrap and scavenged timber. They are the new *perestroika* necessities: family sheds for cattle, chickens, and pigs. Behind them is the main Jona *kartoshka* field, with about a dozen large family plots. Here individual Jona families must grow the food that will keep them going throughout the winter. No one would think to depend solely on the dairy, the reindeer, or the *magazin* now.

As we walk down the muddy track between the sheds, I see an old couple bent over a makeshift board table. They are scorching something with hand-held blowtorches. It is a freshly slaughtered pig. It looks asleep, quietly suffering the indignity of having its hair and snout whiskers singed off. A long, red slash under its ample chin is still dripping blood onto the table and down its wooden legs to the dirt. I ask permission to photograph the scene and am told to go ahead. The couple are glad to pose beside their scorched pig. Yuliya is sad that it had to die and looks away. I am tired. I still have diarrhoea from something I have eaten or drunk. We slowly walk back to my small apartment and I say goodnight to Alya and Yuliya. Across the playground area from my staircase, we notice a slow but steady leak of yellow-brown fluid onto the grass from a tank trailer attached to a tractor. "What is that?" I ask. "It is from the toilets," replies Alya matter-of-factly. After another "goodnight," I return to my bed and prepare for sleep.

Mike

An eighteenth-century drawing of Sami spearing wild reindeer (Leems, 1767).

CHAPTER 7
THE KOLA PENINSULA MAPS

During the month of July 1996, the Sami mapping teams in Lovozero and Jona completed their traditional land-use and occupancy maps. Both teams had conducted their elder and herder interviews in large measure during the period from January to June, before the arrival of the Canadian contingent. Both teams had also taken English language training on their own in preparation for the July mapping charettes. On the day after the Canadians arrived, the work began in earnest. It was decided to prepare the 1:200,000 scale map of the Kola Peninsula showing the Lovozero area first.

LOVOZERO MAPS
The Sami members of the Lovozero team consisted of Andrei Gavrilov (a retired hunter and fisherman), Pavel Fefelov (a former instructor of reindeer herding at Lovozero's vocational school), Nadya Zolotuhina (a teacher of Sami language in elementary school), and Larisa Avdeeva (president of the Lovozero Sami Association). Karim-Aly worked with the Lovozero group, while Mike and Terry went to Jona to launch the mapping exercise with the Jona team members.

Master copies of the Lovozero and Jona maps are included in the map pocket at the end of the book. Readers are invited to review this chapter with the maps unfolded before them.

The following icons were used:
- **ungulates** - elk, domestic reindeer, and wild reindeer
- **fur-bearers** - rabbit, wolf, marten, arctic fox, fox, wolverine, lemming, muskrat, otter, mink, squirrel, weasel, and bear
- **salt and mineral licks**
- **fish** - jackfish, European whitefish, trout, brown trout, grayling, perch, char, sig, salmon, small salmon, three-spined stickleback, and loche
- **water birds** - geese, ducks, loon, swan, seagull, arctic tern, and crane
- **upland birds and raptors** - grouse (willow ptarmigan, wood-grouse, hazel-grouse), eagles, hawks, and owls
- **berries and other food plants** - blueberry, cloudberry, bilberry, red bilberry, and cranberry

- **medicinal plants** - beard lichen, Iceland moss, sphagnum moss, ledum (marsh tea), lichen, midsummer men (live-ever), wild onion, tundra verdure, angelica, excrescence on the birch tree, and juniper bush
- **trees and shrubs** - birch (including dwarf birch), bird-cherry, spruce, pine, willow (including coastal/river-side willow), pussy willow, alder, aspen, and mountain ash
- **trails**
- **traplines**
- **Sami place names**
- **grave sites**
- **other sites** - historic sites, labyrinth structures, sacred places, sacred stones, stone "traffic signs," and forest fire sites
- **buildings** - church, barn, pillar barn, permanent Sami home, portable Sami home, and herder cabin
- **reindeer herding and breeding areas** - winter, spring, summer, and autumn pastures, reindeer farms, reindeer farm boundaries, main seasonal reindeer driving roads, and reindeer slaughtering areas.

Preparation of these icons had begun during the visit of our Sami partners to Canada in November 1995. A workshop was held in Calgary to answer two questions:

1. What plant, bird, and animal species are relevant to the Kola?
2. What are the relevant icons for Sami fixed sites (i.e., labyrinths, historical sites, grave sites, etc.)?

We quickly found out that it would not be possible to answer these questions immediately. First, translation of species names from English to Russian posed a problem, and we had to use Latin scientific names. Second, our partners understandably did not carry a list in their minds of all the various plant, bird, and animal species. They would have to go back and construct a list through discussions with herders and elders. Third, we were effectively working in three languages: Sami (which in Russia has four dialects), Russian, and English. Occasionally there was difficulty finding Russian equivalents of Sami names. Finally, there was the question of how to translate cultural site icons into English. This raised the wider but central issue related to mapping traditional knowledge: namely, how do we take knowledge that is context- and culture-specific and present it meaningfully in another language?

Maria Sergina validates the first Jona map with Tat'yana Tsmykailo.

Aware of these concerns, we resolved to deal with the more mundane and yet essential issues of naming species and sites first, before addressing the wider concerns of intercultural communication. Between November 1995 and June 1996, extensive work was undertaken to prepare both the icons and the interview protocol. This preparation was achieved against a backdrop of a poor postal service and constantly blocked telephone and fax lines. During the Russian elections, communications into the country seemed very tightly controlled. Consequently we had to rely on Leif Rantala in Finland to take correspondence across the border to our Sami partners.

In addition to the above difficulties, we found upon arrival in Russia that we had not prepared icons for three types of seal and an ocean flounder. When coastal Sami mappers Nina Afanas'eva and Nadya Zolotuhina discovered this oversight, they asked Yakov Yakovlev, the resident carving and woodworking instructor at the Lovozero cultural centre, to do something about it. He quickly determined that the marginal strips being scissored from the prepared icon sheets (a necessary task, as each icon had to be cut out separately prior to placement) were more than adequate for the manufacture of new icons. Yakov simply created several identical seal and flounder sketches from scratch in black ink on the strips, and cut them out for application to the map. This was a superb example of the Russian Sami capacity for appropriate technology in the workplace.

After the placement of icons on the larger Kola Peninsula map was finally concluded, Karim-Aly Kassam convened a series of icon pattern analysis sessions. All trainees were asked to consider the completed map and seek patterns or analytic observations for each icon. The following observations were recorded:

I. UNGULATES

Domestic Reindeer - The domestic reindeer follow the same annual migration 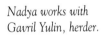 as the elk, motivated by the need to escape the hordes of mosquitoes in the late spring and summer by travelling to the north coast, an area bathed in strong sea breezes. They also are tracked by the bear. Domestic reindeer also eat mushrooms.

Nadya works with Gavril Yulin, herder.

Karim-Aly with the Lovozero team creating the co-management map.

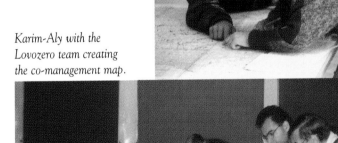

Wild Reindeer - The wild deer are found only in the south of the map area, well below the tree line and away from the reindeer brigade areas. In the winter, the elk and the wild deer share the same territory. The wild deer also favour mushrooms.

Elk - The elk spends its summer on the tundra and its winter just below the tree line. The bear also follows the elk over its range, in a classic predator/prey relationship. Elk especially like to eat mushrooms. Some confusion occurred in mapping the elk range until the Canadian team members learned that the Russian "elk" is called a moose in Canada.

2. FUR-BEARERS

Rabbit - The rabbit is found everywhere on the Kola Peninsula. It does not migrate from the tundra or the forest. Its fur, which is very thin, is generally used only to make caps for children. The Sami eat rabbit meat.

Wolf - Wolves, almost non-existent in the mapped area, are found mainly in the zone between the tundra and the tree line. Andrei Gavrilov noted that in his 20 years of hunting, he had observed a wolf eating reindeer only three times. The Sami systematically trapped wolves to protect their reindeer from predation. In the recent past, if a wolf appeared near a Sami village, all of the hunters would go off in pursuit. The Sami would generally not eat reindeer meat that came from a wolf kill, apparently for fear of contamination. They might eat the lower parts of the legs of a wolf-killed reindeer. Currently wolves are known from the areas of Kandalaksha and Karelia. The Sami used wolf fur, but discarded the meat.

Marten - The marten is actively trapped and hunted, but it is a rare find for the Sami. It too is found in the border zone between tundra and tree line. Marten live in close association with ptarmigan and lemmings. It is thought that marten populations are currently low because of the animal's previous high value as a commercial fur pelt. The Sami hunted marten by blocking their entry hole on the home tree and making a new hole at the bottom of the tree. A fire would be lit next to the new hole, and the marten would be caught (with gloves) when it fell down. In Communist times, trapped marten were sold to the state and were often fashioned into collars on women's coats or made into fur caps.

Arctic Fox - The arctic fox population is seen to be "normal" (a classic Russian term for the desired state of affairs). It eats ptarmigan, lemmings, and reindeer faeces. The arctic fox fur, white as well as silver in colour, was also made into caps and coat collars for women.

Fox - The fox does not eat reindeer faeces but enjoys ptarmigan and lemmings. It is found both on the tundra and in the forest. The fox likes to eat mice and ducks, but not fish. The Sami did not eat its meat, but sold its fur to the state, once again for collars and caps. Fox are very rarely seen nowadays.

Wolverine - The wolverine is found below the tree line only near the mountains and generally in marshy, wet areas. A few individuals are found on the tundra. They too follow the reindeer—not in close proximity like the bear or the wolf, but some 30 to 40 kilometres behind the herd. Wolverine eat reindeer, ptarmigan, and geese. Like the wolf, the wolverine is thought to migrate north from the southern region of Karelia in search of prey. While they may just be very successful at avoiding Sami eyes, it is thought that the wolverine population is smaller than that of the arctic fox. Traditionally the Sami have shot wolverines because they prey on reindeer. A wolverine pelt also found good use as a fur collar or cap.

Lemming - Lemmings are found both on the tundra and in the forest. They are food for fox, arctic fox, wolverine, and bear. Andrei Gavrilov noted that "when the lemming is swimming in the water, it is even consumed by the jackfish." Lemmings are generally loyal to one location, they prefer aquatic areas, and they build up

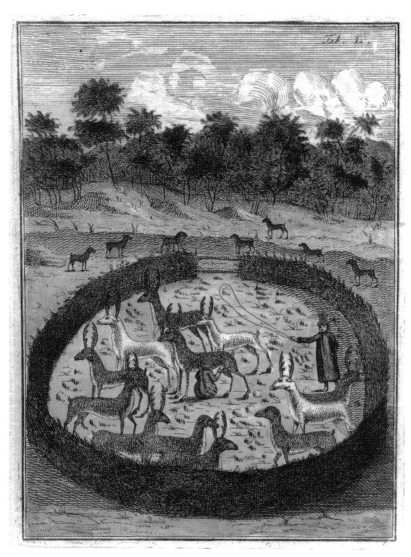

An eighteenth-century reindeer corral (Leems, 1767).

food reserves for the winter. Nikolai Lukin reported that lemming migrations occur near Lovozero about every five years. According to Gavril Yulin, a herder of 28 years' experience, the lemmings in the Lovozero area are prevalent one year and absent the next. In 1996 there were no lemmings to be found, but Gavril expected them again in 1997. He also confirmed Nikolai's observation that they migrate every five years. There is no discernable pattern to their en masse migration.

Muskrat - The muskrat is abundant in marshy, aquatic areas and along river banks. It eats willow, both dwarf and large varieties, and sedge grass. Nowadays the fur is still used to make men's winter caps.

Reindeer and their migratory trail near Lovozero.

55

Otter - The otter (land variety) is an endangered species, and it is against the law to hunt them. Gavril Yulin noted its inclusion in the Red Book, which lists endangered species banned for hunting. Andrei Gavrilov affirmed the pervasive decline of the otter on the Kola Peninsula: in 20 years of hunting, he has seen an otter only twice. Its preferred habitat is lakes and rivers in both the tundra and the forest. Otters eat fish, and especially like salmon and *sig*. Otter pelts are traditionally used for men's caps.

Mink - Mink are found in both forest and tundra, in all seasons and always in aquatic areas. Their numbers are currently high, and they mostly eat fish. Once again they have traditionally contributed their pelts to men's and women's caps. Gavril Yulin recalled that the mink was introduced to the Lovozero region in 1946 to bolster the fur trade.

Squirrel - Squirrels are found only in the forest. They eat mushrooms and pine and fir cones. Their population is said to be normal—in the sense of stable. In 1973-74, Andrei Gavrilov could easily kill 20 per day, as they were unusually plentiful. Their fur is also used for men's and women's caps.

Weasel - Weasels, found both on the tundra and in the forest, are basically aquatic animals. They are reported to have a stable population in the Kola Peninsula. They eat lemmings, and also titmice, ptarmigan, and bird's eggs when available.

Bear - Bears are found on the tundra and in the forest and, as previously noted, follow the migration of the reindeer. The Sami have always hunted bears and eaten their meat. The pelts are generally sold, but some Sami hunters use bear skins as rugs or wall hangings to decorate their homes. Bears also eat elk, wild deer, and all available fish, especially salmon. In the autumn bears eat large amounts of berries and lemmings, if available. The Sami use bear fat for treating burns topically. They make another medicine from the bears' gall bladders, which they sell nowadays to the pharmacy in Lovozero.

3. SALT AND MINERAL LICKS

The Sami reported lick sites along the northern coast of the Kola Peninsula.

 Gavril Yulin maintains that lick sites are used by other ungulates and fur-bearers, as well as by reindeer. In the spring the reindeer especially like to graze on grass that grows through the snow near lakes. This grass tastes salty. In the past, according to Andrei Gavrilov, Sami herders took salt with them to the tundra. He recalls one instance when a reindeer was in such need for salt that it made its way into his *chum* (a tipi-like structure) and consumed salted fish. Currently reindeer are unable to find salt lick sites and suffer greatly from lack of salt. In the spring they often chew each other's horns to satisfy this need.

4. FISH

Jackfish - Jackfish are found in all the lakes and rivers, in both the tundra and the forest.

European Whitefish - This species may be found in all lakes, but the population is reported to be small. However, large populations of European whitefish are found in Umbozero and Lovozero lakes.

Trout - There is little difference between brown trout and regular trout when they are fingerlings, but when they mature they are quite different. Pavel Fefelov noted that "trout are becoming rare because they like very clear water, and this is hard to find in our region."

Brown Trout - Brown trout are more widely known than regular trout and can live in dirty or silty water. They are found in both the tundra and the forest, and even in small lakes.

Grayling - Like the trout, the grayling is found in clean, clear water, often with a stony stream bed. Grayling are found in small rivers and in both large and small lakes. Their habitat zone includes both the tundra and the forest. They lose their taste very quickly after being caught, and must be eaten the same day.

Perch - Perch are widely available except in the high tundra areas.

Char - Char are abundant in tundra rivers and lakes, and in larger lakes in the forest.

Sig - *Sig* are common in the forested regions, but only in the larger rivers in the tundra. They are not found in the high tundra.

Salmon - Salmon are found in most high tundra rivers that connect to the ocean. Salmon are not found in the forest zone in the Lovozero region because they do not come this far south. They do, however, frequent the larger rivers like the Ponoy in the southern Kola region. Salmon have traditionally formed a very important part of the Ponoy Sami villagers' diet.

Three-Spined Stickleback - This fish is common everywhere both in the tundra and in the forest. It is eaten by certain fish species, but not by people. The Russians, but not the Sami, make soup stock from the stickleback.

Loche - The loche is found everywhere, especially in unclear, turbid water. These fish are found in the rivers of the high tundra, and always near the bottom. When the Sami go net fishing and catch loche, it means that the net touched the bottom of the lake or river. Whole loche were eaten in the old days. Now the Sami only make fillets out of them.

Small Salmon - The small salmon is found in the rivers of the eastern Kola high tundra. It is not found in forest region rivers.

5. BIRDS

Geese - Geese are mostly found in the Kola river deltas and river basins.

They also feed, rest, and moult in swampy areas of the tundra. Gavril Yulin noted that today the Sami use the goose for food only, and do not use its feathers. The stomach is considered to be a particular delicacy. In the past, Sami women used a bone from the neck of the goose to hold wool. The wool was rolled onto the bone and kept there to dry. This wool (from sheep that were introduced into the Kola) was used to make woolen stockings for Sami herders.

Ducks - Ducks are common to all aquatic areas in the Kola. The Sami

traditionally collected eggs from nests on islands. Duck feathers are used to make pillows.

Loon - The loon is common across the Kola, and is even found in the High

Arctic areas. It is much rarer than duck species, however. The Sami comment that generally you see only one pair of loons per lake.

Swan - Swans are found in all aquatic areas, but the Sami do not hunt them. They are rare nowadays, and are usually spotted only when they are in flight. According to Gavril Yulin, the Sami hold the swan in special regard. He says, "The swan is like a woman, and the Sami never touch it."

Seagull - Gulls are common all over the Kola, especially along the seacoasts.

Arctic Tern - These birds are found in all lakes and rivers, and especially near the sea. "If the arctic tern has come, we say the summer has arrived," noted Gavril Yulin. The arctic tern is the last bird to migrate north and the first bird to migrate south (in the middle of August).

Crane - Like swans, cranes are generally seen only in flight. They are most common in the west Kola forest area.

Ptarmigan - Ptarmigan are commonplace everywhere. They are eaten by the Sami and by foxes. The stomach of the willow ptarmigan is a *K* delicacy amongst the Sami, like the goose stomach. Sometimes the feathers of the ptarmigan are used for pillows. Gavril Yulin said that Sami mothers collect ptarmigan feathers as dowry for their daughters.

Grouse (includes the wood and hazel grouse) - Grouse are only found in the forest zone. They nest in dry locations, mostly near spruce and pine trees. The tail feathers of the wood grouse are used for decorations.

Eagle - The eagle is broadly distributed throughout the Kola Peninsula, even in the mountainous areas. The Sami classify it as rare, however, and do not hunt it.

Hawks - Hawks are found everywhere, but—like the eagle—are rare. Hawks are known to winter in the Kola. They eat rats and mice, fish, and ptarmigan.

Owls - White owls inhabit the tundra, not necessarily near water areas. They are also found in mountain passes. They hunt at night and sound like a human baby. Normal owls, smaller and grey in colour, are found in the forest only. They too are nocturnal hunters.

6. BERRIES

Blueberry - Blueberries are common to swampy areas, and the Sami describe them as like the bilberry, only softer to the touch. They are eaten raw and made into jam and juice.

Cloudberry - Cloudberries are common, especially in marshy areas. The Sami pick cloudberries in the fall, store them in a barrel underground, and eat them during the winter. Nowadays they are mixed with sugar and stored in the cellars of Lovozero and Jona. Cloudberries may also be cooked with sugar and made into tasty jam. The Sami also make cough medicine out of dried cloudberries.

Bilberry - Similar to a blueberry, the bilberry lasts longer and is used to make jam. The Sami encourage people with poor eyesight to eat dry bilberries. Bilberry juice is also a Sami household staple in season.

Red Bilberry - While not common in the tundra, the red bilberry is frequently found in the forest. Mixed with apples, red bilberries make especially good jam. Bilberry leaves are used to promote urination.

Cranberry - Another common Kola berry, the cranberry, often occurs in such numbers as to "resemble a carpet." Bears love to eat cranberries in the autumn season. The Sami collect cranberries late in the autumn, place them in barrels, and store them in cellars for consumption over the winter. Cranberry juice is often drunk with vodka to lessen the effects of alcohol on the body the next day.

7. MEDICINAL PLANTS

Moss - Moss is not found in the tundra, but only in the tree zone. Moss grows on spruce trees. In addition, **Beard Lichen** is more significant to the reindeer. Beard lichen is black and hangs "like hair" from spruce trees. The reindeer eat this lichen in their winter pastures.

Iceland Moss - Occurring commonly in the tundra, this too is eaten by the reindeer in winter and spring. In the old days, the Sami used it to caulk the windows of their herding cabins.

Sphagnum Moss - Summer is the best time to gather sphagnum moss, which occurs in forests and tundra. It finds ready use as an insulation material: the Sami use it to chink between logs in their tundra and forest cabins. It is also used to treat cuts and scrapes; to make sanitary napkins, baby diapers, and bandages; and, mixed with tobacco, to roll cigarettes. It also prevents mould from growing on berries. Because sphagnum moss is prolific throughout the Kola Peninsula, we decided to map only its harvest locations near villages.

Alder Bark - The bark of the alder is used to treat skin diseases and provide relief from insect bites. The Sami boil the bark in water until it turns red, then wash the wound or affected area with it. The bark is also used in handicrafts, as a reddish-tan dye for reindeer hide.

Marsh Tea - This plant also occurs just about everywhere. On the map, it is shown mostly in tundra harvest sites. When boiled in water and made into a poultice, it is helpful for treating skin diseases. It is best collected in June and early July, when the flowers are not quite developed. "It has also been used to treat diabetes," adds Tat'yana Louk'yanchenko. It can be drunk as tea to cure a common cough, "but beware of its very strong taste," advises Andrei. Marsh tea may have narcotic values, but this has not been scientifically investigated. "If you put it in your nose, you get a headache," explains Nina. It acts like smelling salts.

Lichen - Lichen grows on stones and rock faces in the tundra. It also grows on old trees and cliffs by the sea. The Sami harvest it to use as a dye for wool: it produces beautiful greens and yellows. Reindeer love to eat lichen, especially in the summer and autumn when they are out on the tundra or along the beaches. They will often climb up very steep slopes to access lichen for grazing. In winter, the reindeer climb up above the tree line to graze on lichen in alpine areas.

Midsummer Men - This rather rare plant grows only on the coastline, and the Sami harvest it when it flowers in June. It is used to flavour food and is valued as a strong stimulant. It is "Sami ginger," translates Leif. The ginger taste comes from the roots of the plant. Reindeer do not eat midsummer men.

Wild Onion - Wild onion grows in the tundra, on the shores of lakes and rivers. It is harvested "before it gets too long," at the end of May or beginning of June. By July, the harvest is over. It is a good source of vitamins and can ward off scurvy. It is rich in vitamin C.

Tundra Verdure - This plant occurs around lakes with sandy shores. As the harvest starts in June, tundra verdure is often collected at the same time as bird's eggs. It is used in fish soup, to which it lends a minty taste. The reindeer also eat this tundra plant.

Angelica - Angelica grows around houses in association with grasses. It is harvested in the late spring and early summer (June and July harvest times are best). It is often picked and eaten fresh. You take off the outside "hardest part" first. You can also cook angelica "like meat on the fire." Possibly reindeer eat it as well.

Birch Sap - Birch sap is harvested right off the birch tree and can be boiled for tea. It is said to be good for the liver and the stomach. It will stop vomiting attacks and can be collected at any time of the year. It occurs in birch stands along the tundra rivers and is especially useful in winter.

Juniper - Juniper also grows along riverbanks. The branches are collected for burning in the homes, to freshen the air with its characteristic scent. The bitter juniper berries can be used for cough medicine. Berries are best when harvested at the end of July.

8. SITES AND STRUCTURES

After placing all the tree and shrub icons on the map, we focused attention on the graves, historic sites, and structures associated with reindeer herding and breeding areas.

Sacred Place - The Sami system of religious beliefs includes the cult of the sacred stone. In many sacred places of the Kola, the sacred stone features prominently. In the past, fat and blood were given as sacrifices at the sacred locations; today, money is sometimes used instead. Often the sacrifice is accompanied by a wish.

Sacred Stone - According to our museum guide in Lovozero, a Komi woman, the sacred stone was used for spiritual guidance in bad times and to provide a good omen to hunters and fishers. Often the Sami made sacrifices to the sacred stone. Gavril Yulin noted, "We see all kinds of strange stones there (while herding); we do not pay attention; you have to ask elders about this." The Sami elders are rightly secretive when talking to outsiders about their spirituality. Much information regarding the spirituality of the cult of the stone is now dying with the elders. This is the classic conflict between tradition and modernity, coupled with several centuries of Christianization. It is difficult to gauge the degree to which Sami traditional spirituality exists today. Every family clan had its own sacred stones, which were known only by members of the clan. Today the Sami youth are sceptical about the role of sacred stones. According to Andrei Gavrilov, "In Soviet Russia this kind of information could have been used against you!" He relates a story of how once a group of men had to move a sledge across a ridge by hand. They could not use reindeer power because of the terrain. The sledge was being moved near a sacred stone. While working, the men had been using abusive and profane language, despite warnings from the women. When the night came, the winds rose, and the echoes of their abusive words could be heard hauntingly in the wind.

Labyrinth - Today many labyrinths are covered by plants. Their significance is not known; however, it has been suggested that they may be maps of fishing locations.

Traffic Signs - According to Gavril Yulin, herders use "traffic signs" as direction markers to find their way in poor weather. Built up of large or small stones, and always pyramid-shaped, they vary in size from .5 to 2 metres in height. They are found in many locations, on the tops of hills as well as on lower ground. On lake shores, they are used to indicate where to put fishing nets. The meaning of the traffic sign can now be decoded only by local people who know the terrain. According to Andrei Gavrilov and Nikolai Lukin, the traffic signs appeared during Soviet times and were put there mostly by Russians. The Sami, they maintain, are currently using them for orientation and direction to specific locations in winter.

Fire - The map shows five locations where fires have taken place. Fires damage the precious lichen, which takes many years to grow back. Forest fires are the most difficult to control.

Cabins - This icon indicates the site of a base camp for reindeer herders. Herders leave their families at these camps.

Permanent Sami Homes - These sod houses are no longer used by the Sami. Today, according to Gavril Yulin, poachers are using these traditional Sami homes as overnight camps.

Barn - This traditional storage facility of the Sami is no longer in use. In addition to the barn (or *ambar*), the Sami would also have a *karotozera*, a place where they would store meat and fish to keep it cold. They would salt reindeer, elk, or fish, place the meat in a barrel, and put it into the ground. The Sami continue to practise this method of storage and natural refrigeration today.

Pillar Barns - Another storage facility out of the reach of animals, these "barns on stilts" are no longer in use, and many have collapsed. Those that are still standing are found at the sites of traditional Sami *siidas* (extended family settlements).

Historical Site - The historical site is the location of a traditional Sami *siida*. About 600 ancient Sami settlements have been found in the Lovozero region.

LAND-USE PATTERNS

Noted below are some of the principal land-use patterns observed by the mapping team on the Lovozero map:

- Reindeer herders describe the locations of birds, animals, and plants on the basis of their brigades. Rivers and the tree line actually form the borders that divide their respective herds into brigade units. In the summer, barbed wire fences that run for 30 to 40 kilometres along the rivers are also used to separate reindeer brigades. But in winter these fences, covered by snow, are of little use.
- The tree line also plays an important part in distinguishing the habitats of bird species.
- According to many Sami elders, berries are found in areas sheltered from the wind. Berries are found in both the tundra and the forest regions of the Kola.
- From the size of the Sami *siida* (as revealed by the number of sod houses), it is clear that the Sami were not large-scale herders.
- It is noteworthy that sacred sites, historical sites, and traffic signs are found mostly in the western region of the map. This suggests that the Sami informants have limited knowledge of the east. Knowledge of the landscape east of Lovozero could have been obtained from Sami living further east.

There are nine reindeer brigades organized by the Lovozero Sami and currently used by the Tundra Joint Stock Company, a creation of the new economic era. Once again the Lovozero Sami, along with their Nenets and

Komi neighbours, have the ability to exercise private ownership of reindeer. As Tundra struggles to come to grips with the new economic reality, it clings to some of the old collectivist era terms: the reindeer are allocated to brigades, and each brigade has separate unit areas.

REINDEER HERDING

The following are summary extracts of interviews with three herders from the Lovozero region. All talk about some aspect of reindeer herding. Gavril Yulin is a practising reindeer herder who describes what the lifestyle means to his family, the technological changes that have taken place, and the now constant threat from poachers. He explains, "We herd only to protect the reindeer from predators." There are approximately 6,000 reindeer in his brigade. He and his family, consisting of his wife and their six-year-old son, consume one reindeer a month. He was taught reindeer husbandry by his father. "It is in my blood!" he exclaims. Herding is Gavril's way of making ends meet. The reindeer freely choose grazing areas within their natural brigade boundaries. Over the past 25 years, much has changed in reindeer husbandry. "Before, I used my reindeer as my snowmobile," explains Gavril. "Now I have to buy a snowmobile." Under the Soviet government, he adds, "the helicopter would take us north to the tundra. Now I have to go by foot. The whole system is collapsing." Today the Sami herders have to protect their reindeer not only from animal predators, but also from human poachers. Herders are not allowed to carry rifles according to Russian regulations; poachers, however, have both guns and snowmobiles.[4] While technology has made life somewhat less difficult for the herders, it has made it even easier for the poachers. In December 1995, poachers on snowmobiles, indiscriminately shooting at Gavril's herd, almost shot him. This happened along the coastal region near several military bases.

Andrei Gavrilov describes the migration of reindeer herds and calving. The migration pattern of the reindeer is related to the presence of bears, who follow the herds, and also to the swarms of mosquitoes omnipresent in the summer. In the winter the reindeer rely mostly on lichen; in the summer,

---

[4] However, over the last year (July 1996-97), the regulations have been changed. Now herders are allowed to carry weapons.

mostly on grass—and to a lesser degree on lichen. In the autumn the reindeer also eat mushrooms. The domestic reindeer used for driving can also be fed bread, according to Andrei. At calving time, the herder's day is 24 hours long. The reindeer choose the region midway between the coast and the tree line for calving. This is the first area to become free of snow. During calving season, two or three herders are required to guard the newborns.

Nikolai Lukin, a longtime key informant of Tat'yana Louk'yanchenko, provided a detailed interview on the structure and operations of the old and new brigade systems. Traditionally, each brigade had its own territory and camp. To some degree the new brigades are mixed up, as boundaries have been moved to accommodate the large number of military people in the region. Poaching within the brigade areas is also causing great concern: "Now poachers even come to our tundra cabins and ask for a room!" exclaims Nikolai.

Very few wild reindeer inhabit the tundra zone of the Kola. The Lovozero herders have seen a few in the south of brigade unit 6. The domesticated reindeer migrate north every spring, by instinct, from the treed areas in the south Kola to the tundra and the Barents Sea. They love the offshore breezes and beaches of the coast because here they can escape from the hordes of mosquitoes on the tundra. Their migratory path is plain and straight, and once under way they are impossible to stop. En route, the reindeer browse: "They are not like cows, eating everything," explained herder Pyotr Galkin. Their diet includes winter- and summer-range lichen, moss hanging from trees, mushrooms, and grasses. Calving occurs in the tundra areas that are first free of snow. Small groups of herders are always present during calving to protect the newborns from predators, typically bears and ravens. Soon after the calves are born, the Sami herders make characteristic identifying marks or nicks on the ear of each calf. All of the herders interviewed pointed out that the young reindeer can stand within two or three hours of birth, and after one day of life, they can run on the tundra. Quiet is of utmost importance during calving season, and the best brigade areas are the quietest. They are singled out by the herders as zones for the utmost protection. The best and quietest area is the summer range of brigade number 6. The noisiest area is that of brigade number 9 because of the presence of the military.

In a matter of a year, between July 1996 and July 1997, the conditions of reindeer herding have deteriorated. Andrei Gavrilov explains that herders are having difficulty locating the reindeer herds. "Last year we collected 5,000 reindeer in the region of brigade number 5," he says, "and this year, they could only find 200 animals." In the summer, the reindeer go to the northern coast. In the autumn, they have to be herded to the south, by foot (before the snow) or by snowmobile (after the snow). If the reindeer herds are left on the coast all year round, that pasture land will be wiped out. Many of the snowmobiles do not work, and for the first time snowmobiles from the West had to be purchased.

"The relationship between the reindeer and the herders is breaking down," explains Andrei. "To tame the reindeer again, you have to work 25 hours a day!" There has been a change in the generation of reindeer herders. The older herders do not work anymore; therefore, their reindeer herding knowledge and skills are being lost. The herders of the younger generation lack experience. For example, in the past the herder knew the regions where there was more or less snow. "Today," explains Andrei, "due to the lack of experience, the younger herders do not know." He adds that alcohol consumption and drunkenness have also created problems for herding.

Normally, the slaughter of reindeer is over by the end of December, but last year's slaughter was not completed until the following March. The best-quality meat is obtained from the reindeer that are slaughtered by December. The Tundra Company lost 100 million rubles because they could not slaughter the reindeer in time to fulfill their contract with the Swedish company Norrfrys.

In addition, weak infrastructure support by the Tundra Company is exacerbating the difficulties, explains Larisa Avdeeva, the Lovozero Sami president. Both the Komi and Sami associations have tried to explain the conditions to the Tundra Company, but without much result. The lack of infrastructure support (such as fuel for light and wood for heating) is contributing to the deterioration of reindeer herding.

Together, the problems of alcoholism, a young generation of inexperienced herders, and poor infrastructure support are weakening reindeer herding in the Lovozero region. Another problem may be that the herds are too large for a smaller group of inexperienced herders to manage. In the past, the Sami managed smaller herds (Volkov [1946], trans. 1996:19-23). Andrei predicts, "If the current situation continues, reindeer herding will collapse within the next two to three years."

THE JONA MAPS

The Jona maps, prepared on the same 1:200,000 scale used for Lovozero and the surrounding Kola Sami homelands, also used all of the same icons to denote harvest locations and fixed Sami cultural sites. As in Lovozero, the first icon placed was a reindeer, chosen by the Jona Sami Association president, Tat'yana Tsmykailo. Joining Tat'yana (Tania), Mike, and Terry in Jona were Yuliya Sergina, her father Vladimir, Vladimir's sister Alya Sergina, Valery Sotkoyarvi, and Leif. As in Lovozero, the ethnographic and land-use interviews had preceded the mapping work by several months. "The elders will join us for validation when we are finished," says Tania. As we started the work on July 16, 1996, Leif explained: "The old Sami women[5] do not want to talk to us yet because they are watching their American soap operas on TV."

With a touch of humour, Alya noted at the outset of the mapping that there are really three eras of Sami reindeer stewardship in the Jona homelands:

1. The "Mesozoic Period," from the very beginning of reindeer until 1930. During this time the extended Sami families practised private reindeer herd ownership. On our map, we agreed to encircle the old family areas in orange.

2. The "Stalin Period," from 1930 to roughly 1974.[6] During this time collectivization of reindeer occurred, and the state asserted its herd ownership rights over the wishes of the old extended-family, private-ownership regime. On the map, the "Stalin" reindeer zones were encircled in red.

3. The "*Perestroika* Period," roughly from 1985 to the present. During this period, the old collective farms broke down, and the Jona Sami once again asserted private ownership.

On the map, reindeer zones of this period were circled in green. It was explained that 1974-85 was a period of progressive economic chaos, which saw the beginning of the breakup of the old Soviet state in the Kola Peninsula.

Vladimir noted that most of the bear icons that he was placing on the map were for recent kill sites. Leif responded, "Perhaps each bear icon should

---

[5] Mariya Sergina (73 years old) and Matryona Sotkoyarvi (81 years old).

[6] This date was chosen, even though Stalin died in 1953, to make the point that, for the Sami, his regime in effect continued.

also have a cross beside it," to the general amusement of the mapping team. It was evident that in Jona the current hunting economy is very important. Even though hunting pressure is increasing because of the collapse of orderly food supply to the Jona store, Vladimir asserted that "natural instinct causes more wildlife to be born in times of over-hunting."

When the lemming icons were being placed on the map, the team realized that they did not know where the lemmings went in their cyclical migrations. After some thought, Vladimir interjected: "They must go to Finland when they are starving to death in Russia!"

Alya joked, "There should be an icon for fat dogs in Jona." When asked if her dog was fat, she replied, "No, a fat dog would disappear immediately!"

An anomaly was noted for char: a special kind exists only in very deep lakes, over 60 metres deep, and there are two such lakes on the Jona homelands map.

All of the Jona Sami mappers noted that their principal connections with their neighbours have historically run north-south. Tania explained that they "traditionally had almost nothing to do with the Lovozero Sami." In the "Mesozoic Period," every Sami family had a summer lake and a winter lake to live beside and fish in. "They chose their lakes and rivers as they moved to the area over many centuries," said Tania. There was much family pride attached to these lakes and rivers, and Tania laughingly mocked Vladimir when he put the icon for a small fish in one of her rivers!

Tania further pointed out that all of the Jona Sami housing icons are really for one or two or three families. In the old "Mesozoic Period," young Sami adults basically chose whichever family they wanted to live with when they married. Before collectivization, maternal or paternal grandparents and the nuclear family typically lived together in one house.

During collectivization, the Russian army classified many Sami, along with all Finns in the region, as *kulaks* (agricultural capitalists). Their private reindeer were taken away, along with all fishing gear, and those who complained were shot or sent away to the *gulags*, never to be seen again. Leif Rantala is in fact the first Finn to visit the Jona area in about 110 years.

Collectivization was ultimately unsuccessful in the Jona region, and reindeer herd numbers dropped drastically after 1930. The eventual introduction of a dairy gave the Sami opportunities for new jobs, further weakening their connection to reindeer herding. As economic conditions worsened in the 1990s, the Jona Sami turned more often to gathering foodstuffs available in the bush economy. The detailed Jona map knowledge of gathering sites close to the road system is further evidence of local reliance on berries, wild meat, fish, and edible plants.

The post-1985 "*Perestroika* Period" reflects the offer by Russian authorities of private reindeer once again. The green circles illustrating the new reindeer territories on the map are much smaller than those for the lands allocated during the collectivization of the "Stalin period." Reintroduction of reindeer occurred in 1985 and 1986, when two shipments, totalling some 800 reindeer, were taken in from Lovozero. Prior to their arrival, about 40 kilometres of fencing had been erected, using local timber and discarded fishnets from the Murmansk garbage dump. The new reindeer played havoc with the fencing, and in the spring many were eaten by wolves and bears, or taken by poachers. These predations continue. The new reindeer farm was financed by federal money from Moscow, and the first administrators used some of that money to buy three new cars. Current efforts to re-establish reindeer are not faring well, and only about 300 animals remain.

Tat'yana Louk'yanchenko noted that when she was last in Jona in 1984, just prior to the advent of *perestroika*, no one was fishing for survival purposes. Now survival fishing is very important to Jona. She also noted that there were about 800 cows at the dairy in the early 1980s; now, about 150 remain.

After the Jona mapping was completed, both Mariya Sergina and Matryona Sotkoyarvi came to validate the maps. Small changes and additions were made to the work as a result of their suggestions, and they announced their pleasure that the work had been undertaken so completely. We gave each of them a tin of Finnish reindeer meat as a gift, and both said it had been a long time since they had eaten Sami reindeer.

CHAPTER 8
SACRED SITES AND PROFANE ACTS:
A DAY FROM MY DIARY

July 18. It is 7 a.m., and I did not get a good night's sleep. I am excited about our work; it is reaching completion, and I am worried about being able to get it out of Russia. Will the military guards at the border checkpoint look at the maps? Will they take them away? If they do, what will happen to the Sami? The maps contain details of Sami sacred areas, hunting sites, and fishing locations. The military will learn the location of the calving areas of the reindeer. Losing the maps might mean not only losing our years of collaborative work, but actually causing further harm to the Sami.

We are starting late because Pavel's alarm clock did not go off and Nikolai, our cook, had to walk to his apartment to wake him up. Larisa says, seeking to control her obvious irritation, "His ex-wife must have visited him last night." When he did arrive, we had to wait for him to put his fishing nets into the boat. He will cast them while we hike to the sacred sites. I am concerned whether his boat is actually seaworthy!

All three boats are finally geared up to go. We will travel east of Lovozero to North Salma, a narrow strait on a vast lake. This area is said to be a site used by Lovozero Sami as a fishing camp and a graveyard. Three days ago, Tat'yana Louk'yanchenko, the Russian ethnologist and our project partner, gave me a copy of her article on the burial customs of the Kola Sami before leaving with Michael for the village of Jona. According to her, the Sami settlements coincide with cemeteries. Often Sami camps were accompanied by their own cemeteries. These camps, which were associated with specific activities such as hunting and fishing, tended to be occupied seasonally, in spring, summer, autumn, or winter. In addition, cemeteries tend to be located on dry, high ground "beyond water." The custom of burial beyond water is connected with the belief that water acts as an effective barrier, preventing the dead from returning to the world of the living (Louk'yanchenko, 1983). The idea that death involves crossing over water is common among many societies around the world. The notion of using water as an effective barrier, Dr. Louk'yanchenko maintains, is from a fear of the dead. The dead cannot return across the water, so that the living should no longer fear them.

The dilapidated grave of a young Sami girl.

We have landed on North Salma and I have just taken pictures of some grave sites. Very little remains, and the graves have collapsed. I am told this is the grave of a little girl. It is noteworthy because her body was sewn into a shroud of birch bark. At the time of her death, she was apparently wearing leather shoes and adorned with jewellery typical of Sami workmanship. We are told that forty years ago, when Russian archaeologists first exhumed the bodies, these graves were in much better shape. Today they are dilapidated and covered with considerable growth. Nowadays Russian tourists and the military come to this area to fish. They use the wood from these grave sites to supply fires for their campsites. We walked across several campsites with bottles of Stolichnaya vodka thrown nearby.

Karim-Aly protected from mosquitoes on the trek to the sacred lake.

A meal on the shore.

I have now walked back to where the old Sami fishing camp was located—at a safe distance from the graves, on the other side of this narrow strait. We are about to have our breakfast, and Larisa has asked me to wash my hands. Bewildered by the motherly behaviour of my Sami colleague, who is not much older than I am, I ask why. In a matter-of-fact way she says, "We have just visited a grave site. You always wash your hands afterwards!" It had nothing to do with the fact that I had soaked the exposed parts of my limbs with enough bug spray to sustain the price of this chemical on the international market for a year. It was not because she wanted me to remove this mosquito repellent from my hands before eating.

As I chew on some bread and cucumbers and sip hot tea, Larisa begins a legend about North Salma. Once upon a time, Liaine, a Sami man, had gone hunting with his son and brother. While they were gone, the Sami camp was attacked by a group of Chuds,[7] who killed most of the Sami and took Liaine's wife, Voavr, prisoner. Liaine's brother's wife managed to escape and swim to an island (in Sami called "Safe Island") to seek help. In the meantime, the Chuds tied Voavr's foot so that she would not escape.

When Liaine returned with his brother Aripi and son Peairi, he found the Sami camp smouldering and empty. They followed the tracks and, not too far away from the destroyed settlement, they found the Chuds' camp.

The Chuds were too large a group to engage in direct battle, so the three men returned to the forest. They decided that they had to use their intelligence rather than brawn if they were going to succeed in freeing Voavr.

While her husband, son, and brother-in-law worked out a plan, Voavr was ordered to cook for the Chuds. Being a good cook, she prepared reindeer meat in a manner that would rival the culinary skills of any Chud woman. As the Chud captain sat in his *chum* slicing and consuming a big piece of meat prepared by Voavr, Liaine managed to climb to the top of the tipi. Looking down through the opening, he saw the captain holding the meat in his mouth while slicing pieces with his knife. Liaine shot an arrow. It hit the knife, which then went through the mouth and into the throat of the Chud captain,

---

[7] It is noteworthy that in many legends of the Lovozero Sami, Chuds are portrayed as the antagonists. Perhaps "Chuds" is a generic term for a group of southerners invading northern lands.

killing him. Liaine and the others, using their bush skills, then killed the Chud invaders one by one.

We are back on the boat and heading to Seidozero, the sacred heartland of the Lovozero Sami. Seidozero means "the Lake of the Sacred Stone." We are now in open water and—typically—Pavel's boat is not with us. Pavel's boat has Nina Afanas'eva, the president of the Kola Sami, and Nikolai, our cook: two good reasons for not going any further. As the two boats wait for them to arrive, Sergei, Larisa's husband, starts to fish. We just caught a *sig* (a fish common in these lakes). Overhead a low-flying helicopter passes, carrying Western tourists to fish for salmon on the Ponoy River. The Sami, however, can no longer fish in their own river, because it is now being rented out to a Finnish-American tourist outfit. So much for *perestroika*!

Andrei in the next boat has just caught a fish. He shouts, "The ground is too heavy. I cannot lift it up." The fish gets away. Pavel's boat is now in sight, and we continue to Seidozero.

An hour and a half later heading southwest, we land. Now we begin a three-kilometre uphill walk to the Lake of the Sacred Stone. Today anybody can walk into this once-secret location. There is no money to enforce any laws. Looking at the map one can see why this isolated area has sacred resonances for the Sami. Historically, the Lovozero Sami came here for their summer festival in mid-July. The river that connects Seidozero and Lovozero lake is called Seidiok in Sami.

As we hike to Seidozero, Andrei peels off some spruce sap from the tree. "It cleans the teeth and freshens the breath," he says. "To boot, it changes colour while you chew, so it is interesting to look at!"

At last we have arrived at the Lake of the Sacred Stone. According to Sami tradition, I have just thrown a silver coin into the water and a copper coin onto the land. Two teenagers who were accompanying us, Anna and Sasha, have gone missing. Sasha is Larisa's son, and Anna is Nadya's daughter. In addition to the two mothers, Pavel has gone to look for them. We wait at a hunter's cabin for the search party to return. According to Andrei, "amateur" hunters come here to hunt the fox, grouse, ptarmigan, and mink. There is irritation in his voice because they are intruding on sacred Sami land.

The mosquitoes surround us like a swarm of bees. Nina Afanas'eva has lit a fire to get rid of them. It works when you are close to the fire, and particularly to the smoke. Otherwise, I continue to use massive amounts of bug spray. This is the first time Nina, the president of the Kola Sami, has come to the Lake of the Sacred Stone.

Pavel has found the children, but now the mothers are missing. We decide to continue our hike along the lake towards the sacred cliffs. Pavel will remain behind with the children and bring the mothers to where we are going. This part of the hike is challenging because of the muskeg and the marsh. The creek is hard to cross, but nobody wants to give up.

We are back at the shore of the lake, and this time the sacred cliffs are in full view. The stone is very important to the Sami; it is among the most sacred objects. The phrase "cult of the stones" has been used to describe their religious practices. Dr. Louk'yanchenko suggests that sacred stones (*sieidi* in Sami), which are religious monuments, may indeed be grave markers. Andrei relates a personal encounter with *sieidi*. When Andrei was a child, his family had gone fishing. On their way, they passed a sacred stone on the shore of the lake. They rowed past the sacred stone on their way to the rich fishing grounds. They caught nothing. His mother made cutlets of fish liver and eggs, returned by boat to the sacred stone to give them as an offering, and then they caught lots of fish! The sacred stone seems to be where people go to get their needs and wishes fulfilled. Both Nina and Andrei pick up stones from the shore and give them to me as a gift. I thank them and save them for my daughter Tahera. I cannot wait to tell her about this journey.

Larisa, Nadya, Pavel and the two children have all arrived.

There are two islands within the Lake of the Sacred Stone, just in front of the cliffs. On the larger of these two islands are the graves of shamans: the greatest among them are buried here. Once a year, at the time of the summer feast, the Lovozero Sami would travel to the islands. They would wash themselves in these sacred waters. Among the rituals, the men would go to the islands on the lake, undress, put reindeer horns on their heads, and wrestle to determine the strongest. While the men were on the islands, no women were supposed to be present. The winner would have the right to choose the most beautiful girl amongst the Sami for a mate. The Sami concept of beauty, which included both household and craft skills, is exemplified in the fine handiwork on a young woman's dress. According to the following legend, there have been many battles fought here between the Sami and the Chud,

An impression of an upside-down man on the cliffs (Leems, 1767).

enemies from Scandinavia.[8]

Once upon a time, there was a powerful Sami shaman named Pialk (which in Sami means "big finger"). Pialk fought a Chud leader named Kuiva. The battle was long, and many Sami lives were lost. Pialk used all his power to defeat Kuiva. Finally, mustering all his strength, he threw Kuiva across the lake onto the cliffs, where he turned into stone.

Pointing to the cliffs, Larisa shows me in the natural rock occurrences the shape of a giant man suspended like a cross. The Chud leader, Kuiva, had a fat cook, whom Pialk also turned into stone. Today the cliff looks rounded because of the cook's obesity. Having been wounded in battle and used up all his energy, Pialk the shaman could not turn himself into a mountain. Instead, he turned into a stream (called Vuei).

In these mountains, says Larisa, are many sacred sites. The elders refuse either to talk about them or to reveal their location. According to many Sami elders, Pialk lived at the source of the river that begins in Seidozero.

Nadya relates another tale, told to her by her grandmother. Once upon a time, two men fought for the hand of a beautiful Sami woman. One of them was an evil shaman; the other was a handsome young man. The shaman prepared two wooden cups, each containing a water-like liquid. The liquid in one cup would make the drinker strong and quick. The liquid in the other cup would make the drinker weak and slow. After the wrestling match between the two men had commenced, the shaman asked to stop to have a drink of water. He drank from the cup containing the potent liquid, whilst the young man drank the other. Soon, as they commenced again, it became apparent that the young man was growing weaker. The beautiful young woman, noticing this change, carefully switched the cups. When the shaman called for a break to drink water again, he drank from the wrong cup and grew weak. The young man defeated the shaman and won the heart of the beautiful young woman.

---

[8] Note the recurrence of the Swede invader called Chud (*Tjude*) in Sami tradition. It seems "Swedes" could also be used generically, to mean "Scandinavians." From listening to Larisa, one gets the distinct impression that these battles are embedded in the history of the Sami. According to Odd Mathis Haetta (*The Sami: An Indigenous People of the Arctic*, 1996), these storied events refer to "real incidents" of raids on the Sami by various groups from the 1200s to the 1400s. Unlike Larisa, however, Haetta argues that this group of raiders came from the East.

After a suitable rest, we hike back to our boats, tired and hungry. It is now time for a late lunch, so we are expecting a large meal. Fish has been caught and cooked over the fire. Nikolai has prepared soup. We laugh, grow tired of the mosquitoes, and eat heartily. Nadya reminds us that we need to leave the sacred area before 6 p.m. Otherwise, the spirits will haunt us.

It is now 6:20 p.m., and we are on the boat returning to Lovozero. The water is choppy, and I am finding it hard to write. I have had a wonderful time. I have been treated like family and feel that I have been among family. The mapping has been completed, and I am ready to return home. Three days are left in Russia and three more in England. I will sleep well tonight!

Karim-Aly

CHAPTER 9
THERE IS A MAP AND MORE IS COMING

An article by A. Kuznetsova in *Lovozerskaya Pravda*, Friday, August 9, 1996, translated by Olga Mladenova.

For ten days, the Centre of National Culture was transformed into a research laboratory. In the middle of the hall is a huge table, piled with black-and-white and colour maps and files of materials. The group of enthusiasts who are creating the first Sami map of the Kola Peninsula (and in particular of the Lovozero region) surrounds the table. Some of them speak in English, others in Russian; but they work in harmony. Executive Director and Professor Michael Robinson, Research Associate Terry Garvin, and Theme School Director Karim-Aly Kassam are all from the Arctic Institute of North America at the University of Calgary. Their partners (and that is the term which the guests used to refer to Lovozerians) are N.A. Zolotuhina, P.F. Fefelov, A.S. Gavrilov, and L.P. Avdeeva.

Our readers probably recall that *Lovozerskaya Pravda* already informed them about the joint Sami project, which includes the compilation of a map;

A July Sunday morning in Lovozero.

but things are not as simple as they appear to be at a first glance.

Imagine a situation: you are given a large map and lots of tiny symbols which you have to paste on the right spot. If the symbol represents a medicinal plant, it has to be pasted where the plant grows, and so on. Many things are mapped: plants and berries, animals and fish, sacred places, and various other items which allow us to understand the life of the aboriginal people. Difficult, isn't it? But the mapping activity itself comes at the end. It is preceded by prolonged collection of data.

"That's exactly how it was," says Larisa Avdeeva. "After the visit to Canada, we got together with a group of knowledgeable Lovozerians and spent half a year collecting information. We worked with books, atlases, and maps. We made a list of the oldest reindeer herders (40 persons), divided it among the four of us, and started interviewing them according to our plan. We were glad to discover that our plan and the protocol prepared by the University of Calgary turned out to be very similar. That is probably why our guests were surprised to see how many materials we had already collected, and how easy it was to continue the work. One can only admire the elders' knowledge of the tundra."

"Our group sent to Canada lists of relevant plants, berries, mushrooms, birds, and animals, information about seasonal pastures, reindeer driving roads, bases, scientific stations, marking them with our own symbols, e.g., a traffic sign in the tundra can be a stone placed on the top of another stone or a grave site. The Arctic Institute, on the other hand, has spent ten years doing research on the problems of the aboriginal nations, and therefore had a number of symbols at its disposal. An artist prepared beautiful computerized replicas of our symbols, which we received just a week before the arrival of the University group. For better understanding, we had to organize an English language course."

It now became clear how easily communication was achieved. One should not forget to mention the help provided by the well-known Leif Rantala and Zhenia Yushkov. The Canadian guests confessed that the media furnished only negative information about our country, so it took courage to come. Michael Robinson and Terry Garvin spent four days in Lovozero before going to Jona. Karim-Aly Kassam stayed to complete the map work in Lovozero. The Lovozerians addressed them simply as Mike, Terry, and Karim. The Canadian democratic spirit is transmitted already by this simple form of address. It tremendously facilitates communication and makes it friendly without stressing differences of rank and age. The work routine was strict: the group worked until late at night, with no days off. The first black-and-white working map with lots of symbols on it was prepared. Then all the information was transferred onto a colour map. It had to be ready by July 19, when Lovozerians were invited to look at it and perhaps introduce corrections and additions. Three copies of the map will be prepared. Two (a black-and-white and a colour map) will remain in Lovozero; the third will be taken to Calgary, where it will be used in preparing the project book.

The guests met with the reindeer herders, discussed the maps with them, and were pleased with what they heard. They highly appreciated the preliminary work done by the Lovozero group, which had to interview informants born in 1916, 1917, 1929, and 1936 who lived in various Sami villages. The interviewers each had a black-and-white map on which to note everything they heard.

IS THE CLOUDBERRY A BERRY OR A MEDICINE?

How should we mark it? This question was raised by the group, and Karim weighed the situation carefully before trying to respond to it. There were many such episodes during those ten days. Many technical details were brought up, and decisions were made collectively.

"My job with the partners in Lovozero," says Karim, "is to take care that all symbols are correctly plotted on the map. The ethnographic information has to be complete. The map belongs to the Sami. My duty is to satisfy myself that the mapped symbols correspond to reality. At the end I also have to make sure that the collected information (i.e., the map) is preserved. We expect that there might be difficulties at the Russian customs, but we hope that our project will be understood properly."

"I have done similar work in the North of Canada, in the Himalayas, and in Syria, and I am glad that I had the opportunity to visit you. For a number of years now, society and the aboriginal nations have decided upon the priorities in the usage of natural resources in Canada. It is good that some steps are taken in the same direction in Russia as well."

"In the heads of herders and elders is preserved 'a book.' It is my duty to represent its contents in a scholarly fashion. But the authors of the book are the simple wise folk, whose knowledge and experience have been verified by time. One has to look at it philosophically, and life will then take a turn for the better. When we finish our work on the map, we'll discuss how it can be used."

It was obvious that Karim worked harmoniously with his Lovozerian partners. They gave the impression that they had known each other for a long time. I could not abstain from the traditional question: how did he like it in Russia? And this is what he told me:

"These are difficult times for Russia, we know that. It is good that the Russians' sense of humour helps people out. Foreigners are not easy to get along with, but we do our best not to interfere with the usual course of life with our presence, not to be a nuisance."

"Russia's greatness is in its spirituality. This is the land of Dostoevsky, Tolstoy, Pushkin, Chekhov, Tchaikovsky, Pasternak... Tell me which American is as famous as they are? The Russian people are communists, not capitalists; they follow their own path. It is difficult to live today, but there is hope...?"

Russian kartoshka *in Lovozero.*

FORTY-FIVE YEARS WITH THE ABORIGINALS

Terry Garvin has devoted many years to the problems of the aboriginal nations. He conducts interviews about various aspects of the life of those people whose land was developed by the newcomers. And that means that he is friendly and competent.

Terry is the author of a remarkable book, *Bush Land People*. The earliest photo in the book goes back to 1954. The contents of the book and its production quality are evidence of respect for the aboriginal nations of Canada. Terry told us that most questions regarding the management of natural resources in Canada are dealt with by taking into account aboriginal peoples' opinions and knowledge, and that is to everyone's advantage. Canadians have been using maps like the Lovozero one for many years. School children use such maps as textbooks. The exploration of natural resources should not interfere with the harmony of nature. This is of paramount importance if we are to continue living on our planet.

PARTICIPATORY ACTION RESEARCH

Those were the words used by the Director of the Arctic Institute, Mike Robinson, to denote the methodology for the work of his group. He gives priority to the Sami project and devotes to it all his free time. I asked Mike to tell us how the Sami map can be employed.

"If a construction project is planned for the Jona homelands, the map can help decide on its best location. It can also be used for decision making with regard to the exploration for natural resources. For reindeer calving in the tundra, for instance, silence and peace are essential. That means that there should be no industrial road in the calving area. Reindeer breeding is a traditional occupation for the Sami, and this should be taken into account."

"In northern Canada, much exploration for oil and gas has occurred, and the companies wanted to extract them. But there were Inuit whale hunting sites nearby. An aerial photo was made, and the Eskimo hunters pointed out the whales in the bay. It became clear that the spilled oil and the noise which can accompany exploration might destroy both the whales and the Inuit culture. So, the exploration plan for the bay was abandoned."

Such mutual understanding between society and the business world is admirable. Our examples are mostly negative, and Mike, seeing my reaction, remarked:

"We'll never achieve anything if we don't do our best. After all, the longest trip begins with the first step..."

I asked about the funding of the project. Its duration is two years, and its

Potatoes for the coming winter.

total cost is Cdn $100,000. The majority of the money is spent on travel and living expenses. All participants in the project will receive a small allowance (Cdn $14 per day).

The funding for the project comes from the University of Calgary-Gorbachev Foundation (Mr. M.S. Gorbachev is a former president of the USSR). He earned a nice sum of money by lecturing in Canada and, with the University of Calgary, founded a Trust Fund to encourage cooperation in the scientific sphere, the exchange of experience, etc. Our sincere thanks, Mikhail Sergeevich.

The map will be ready in September or October 1996, and will then be presented to the Oblast administration. An official demonstration of its use will take place in Lovozero as well.

CHAPTER 10
PERESTROIKA AND THE PONOY

The struggle for cultural survival of the Sami across northern Europe is well documented. Policies of "Norwegianization" or "Swedification" have been the hallmark of the Sami's imperial experience. The twin policies of industrialization and Christianization are common features of colonial experience of indigenous people throughout the world. As in the case of aboriginal cultures in North America, Australia, and New Zealand, policies of cultural assimilation extended to banning the usage of indigenous language, enforcing Christianization, establishing an educational curriculum alien to Sami life, and forcing the settlement of nomadic people. Northern European countries had a variety of justifications for such policies. The argument of cultural superiority was certainly widely held by the Norwegians and Swedes. Sovereignty was another justification of assimilation policies. How could a nomadic people, who do not recognize borders, be loyal to the concept of a nation-state based on religion and ethnicity? Perhaps the most convincing justification for assimilation and settlement was that it allowed the governments to appropriate traditional Sami lands in the 1900s (Sami Instituhtta, 1990).

However, the policy of assimilation was skewed to favour the ethnic Finns, Swedes, and Norwegians, because it meant assimilation of Sami resources and exclusion of the Sami people from participation in the mainstream. A vulgar form of social Darwinism was applied. The Sami, unlike other citizens of the state, were prevented from owning land. Furthermore, true to the tradition of colonial paternalism, it was decided to limit their socioeconomic activities to reindeer herding (Sami Instituhtta, 1990). In Sweden, for instance, the school system placed Sami children at a lower educational level in comparison to the ethnic Swedish children (Svonni, 1996).

Like the Sami in northern Europe, the Native communities in the Northwest Territories of Canada encountered a similar fusion of Church and State in education and social policy in the 1920s to the 1940s. The Roman Catholic and Anglican churches were the first to establish schools in the Canadian North. Their educational policy mirrored the policy towards the Sami in Europe. The Native Canadians had to be settled and yet draw a living from their traditional lifestyle. The education of Native children in

Air quality.

this period terminated at grade six, providing only basic reading and writing skills. Little effort was made to give Native children a choice of future employment opportunities by equipping them to enter the wage economy through industrial or government employment. This happened despite the fact that the Native people were best suited to participate in certain activities because of their knowledge of their land and its natural resources (Arctic Circular, 1952: Conference on Eskimo Affairs; Dickerson, 1992; Kassam, 1994).

Both these examples indicate the general pattern of assimilationist policies towards indigenous communities in the global North and the insidious nature of assimilation. This type of partial assimilation is perhaps more repulsive than outright cultural genocide because it reflects a willed effort to undermine indigenous cultures, yet nominally preserve them through political and economic dependence, so as to permanently show the weakness of the indigenous culture in contrast to the European. The scars of this form of cultural apartheid are deep and often incomprehensible.

In contrast, the Sami in Russia may have faced a much more tolerant policy in the 1900s because they resided in a multiethnic state. Taxation

A smelter on the Kola tundra.

chronicles of the 12th and 13th centuries describe Russian settlements being established in the northern regions of the Kola as a result of failed harvests and famine in the South (Volkov [1946], trans. 1996:120; Sami Instituhtta, 1990:33). The Czar's tax collectors followed settlers all the way to the Kola Peninsula. Ironically, these types of records, which convey historical information about the Sami, are also documentary evidence of a means used to establish Russian control over small-scale northern communities. On the other hand, there is evidence from the 16th century of the Czar's providing relief from taxation to the Sami who complained about their tax burden.

Like the Swedes, Norwegians, and Finns, the Russians also promoted their brand of Christianity and language. To prevent Norwegian and Finnish settlements in the Kola, the Czars favoured Russian and Karelian settlers from the era of first contact to the beginning of the 19th century.

Traditionally Sami settlements (*siida*) were organized along the lines of each family's seasonal use of hunting, fishing, and reindeer herding lands. These areas differed from season to season. With the coming of Russian settlers (called the Pomors) starting in the middle of the 15th century, Sami settlements were displaced by the construction of non-Sami towns (Rasmussen, 1995).

Sami life manifested tremendous diversity between hunting, fishing, and reindeer husbandry. Within the herding culture, some families owned herds, while others did not. A minority of families owned herds as large as 500 to 1,000 head. However, the majority of the families owned approximately 100 head (Rasmussen, 1995:49).

A further and more dramatic marginalization of the Sami began in 1887 when the Komi, accompanied by their Nenets herdsmen, migrated to the Kola Peninsula with large reindeer herds each numbering about 5,000 animals. As a result, the diversity of *siida* living underwent permanent change. The Komi were escaping a reindeer disease epidemic in their homelands, along the river Izhma east of the Kola Peninsula. The impact of this in-migration on Sami land resources was that it changed the nature of husbandry. Up to this time, Sami reindeer had run wild, with a minimal presence by the herder most of the year, and were only gathered for the autumn slaughter. The arrival of larger herds meant more competition for grazing land for the Sami, and more intensive use of the tundra. The Komi, unlike the Sami and Nenets, are not a nomadic people. The Sami lifestyle of mixed hunter-gatherer herding is more suited to an ecological balance of resource use. In contrast, the Komi's more intensive (and therefore more economically profitable) style of reindeer herding leads to resource depletion. In effect, this competition internalized a conflict between the Komi and the Sami.

FEATURES OF THE TRADITIONAL SAMI HERDING STYLE INCLUDE THE FOLLOWING:

- free pastures[9] (whereas the Komi treat their reindeer like cattle, with defined pasture areas)
- a summer migration north across the tundra to the Barents Sea
- much smaller herds, with a maximum of about 2,500 reindeer
- the burning of moss to keep mosquitoes away from herds

---

[9] According to N.N. Volkov (1946, trans. 1996:19), in the free pasture system, a herdsman looks after the reindeer in the early autumn, winter, and spring. In the autumn the reindeer are gathered, in the winter they are observed, and in the spring they are measured. Only in the summer months do they roam free. Since reindeer tend to remain in a certain location, the herder is able to find them come autumn.

- using skis or walking while tending to herds (the Komi used sledges)
- the practice of ecologically balanced husbandry.

The final blow to the traditional Sami *siida* came with the Soviet collectivization of reindeer herding and fishing. By 1930, only two years after the first cooperatives were established, more than half of the herds had been collectivized (Rasmussen, 1995). Collectivization resulted in the implementation of the more economically profitable and intensive Komi approach to herding. Reindeer brigades that comprised Komi, Sami, and Nenets herders were created. Today some features of Sami herding, such as free pasturing in the summer and the autumn slaughter for market, are coming back. However, as a result of colonization, a significant portion of the Sami in both Jona and Lovozero do not have access to reindeer herding as a source of livelihood. Sami culture and language are intimately linked to reindeer herding: cultural survival depends on mutually reinforcing connections between reindeer herding and the language. The loss through forced settlement and collectivization of the ability to practise reindeer husbandry in Sami communities translates into loss of the language, which is intimately linked to a reindeer pastoral culture (Svonni, 1996; Kazakevitch, 1997). In turn, loss of language results in loss of herding knowledge. Thus a plea for reindeer herding is a plea for cultural survival. Maintenance of a dynamic Sami culture cannot be separated from reindeer herding.

Many personal tragedies are associated with collectivization and the resistance. Families who resisted collectivization faced forced labour or even death at the hands of the State. Many Sami recall that their fathers disappeared or were given long prison sentences. In the 1930s, 34 Sami and Komi were accused of wanting to form a separate republic. They were given long prison terms or simply executed. Prison meant that many were forced to build the railway, work as labourers, and live in concentration camps called *gulags*. Various forms of repression continued until Stalin's death in 1953.

During World War II, the Sami fought on Russia's northern front. They formed reindeer transport brigades, taking supplies and weapons north and bringing the wounded Russian and Sami soldiers south. In the winter months, the reindeer were the key means of transport. The Sami also participated in the liberation of Norway.

Today the Sami population in Norway, Sweden, Finland, and Russia

Sami elders.

numbers approximately 51,000. The Kola Sami account for only 2,000 (see the following table).

Sami Population Today	
Norway	30,000
Sweden	15,000
Finland	4,000
Russia	2,000
Total	**51,000**
Source: Rasmussen, 1995:48	

With the collapse of the Soviet empire, the lives of the Sami and Komi have yet again been dramatically affected. This time the Russians, Komi, and Nenets, along with the Sami, face a common foe: a chaotic new economy characterized by

Eighteenth-century drawing of bolting reindeer and a wolf (Leems, 1767).

- unemployment
- unpaid wages or pensions for over a year
- poaching on a massive scale
- poor law enforcement
- increasing concentrations of industrial pollutants
- unrelenting breakdown of public infrastructure (water, sewage, heating, etc.)
- takeovers by foreign companies of Sami traditional resources
- destruction of both renewable and nonrenewable resources.

Perestroika was the word former Soviet president Gorbachev used to describe his radical policy for economic change, which resulted in wide-scale adoption of the market system. *Perestroika* means "rebuilding." One can argue, however, that the penetration of the market system into the Kola Peninsula has instead brought further dismantling of what used to be considered positive, and enhancement of what was considered negative. The laws that protected the Sami sacred sites and lands are no longer enforced (Larisa Avdeeva, pers. comm. 1996). Instead, many members of the *nomenclatura*—the old Communist elite—have remade themselves as entrepreneurs. Arguably, it is this elite that controls the resources, and the proverbial "invisible hand" seems to work in an upward direction, lining the pockets of the few while leaving little, if anything, for the masses.

Perhaps the most visibly tragic manifestation of the market system gone wild has been its effect on the veterans who defended the Russian motherland during the war: they are forgotten by the state, do not receive their pensions, and often starve to death. And the general condition of the military is so pathetic that weapons and high-tech equipment are often traded for food or much-needed cash.

The unemployment rate in the county of Lovozero is conservatively estimated at 60 per cent (Rantala, 1995:58). Thus the bush economy sustains many, and poaching is rampant. However, this solution presupposes that people have access to equipment to go hunting, and, in fact, have the bush skills to be successful. Increasingly, the families of those who have both equipment and skill are better able to survive. In a context where most of Lovozero's 3,500 inhabitants rely on the bush economy for sheer survival, the pressure on animal and fish species will ultimately lead to ecological disaster.

Reliance on the bush economy presumes accessibility. Today the Sami are restricted from fishing in their traditional rivers unless they purchase licences. There are 65 salmon rivers in Sami territories within the Murmansk province. The Sami have a licence to fish in only one, for an annual fee of 15 million rubles. Many of the traditional Sami rivers are being leased to foreign companies. The largest salmon river, the Ponoy, has been leased to an American/Finnish company, G. Loomis Outdoors Adventure, which caters to foreign sports fishermen. At one time the Sami could depend upon harvesting 40 to 80 tonnes of fish per annum from this river,[10] but they now do not have any access to it. Instead, wealthy American, Scandinavian, and German fishing clients enjoy the Ponoy at the expense of the Sami (Nina Afanas'eva, pers. comm.). The quotations below are taken from a promotional video from G. Loomis Outdoors Adventure:[11]

- "I think [the Ponoy] is a paradise for fishing... it is full of salmon. I have never seen so many salmon in my life."
- "The Ponoy River is *exclusively at our disposal*, the Ponoy River being about 300 miles long, allows us to spread the beats so far apart that we measure our beats in miles. You can fish all day, never duplicate water throughout your whole week's stay, and never see another person on the river."
- "You will be greeted by our helpful and amiable staff, who will assign you separate rooming accommodations. Each of these American-made tents is equipped with *every possible amenity* right down to electric baseboard heating. Each tent has two beds with *extra*-long and *extra*-wide foam and sleeping bags with ample pillows. The tents have a wooden floor, built-in shelving, and a cozy Finnish wood-burning stove for the chilliest nights. The entire camp has *full electric power*. There are six showers with *plenty* of hot water available *instantly*. The Ponoy camp is simply superb, especially considering how far from *civilization* you are."
- "No one else from the outside *world* is allowed to fish *our* river's beat except our guests. Unlike some Kola rivers, *locals* are not allowed to fish the

---

[10] Leif Rantala (pers. comm.) reports that there were harvests of 59 tonnes in 1934 and 155 tonnes in 1939.

[11] Copy in the files of the Arctic Institute of North America, Calgary, Alberta.

Pavel Fefelov and the tank track ruts on the fragile tundra.

Ponoy. Standing out as the best of all Kola rivers, the Ponoy presents a remarkable combination of attractive *size* and amazing *numbers* [of salmon]."

- "It's *new water*. Nobody has had an opportunity to fish this water before."

The relative splendour and excessive American-style comfort of the camp are juxtaposed to the town of Lovozero, whose 3,500 women, men, and children do not have enough food to eat. Nor do they enjoy heating or hot showers, because the township does not have the funds to fuel their heating plants. This is stark and emphatic testimony to the so-called "victory" of the market system.

The reference to "new water" bears a striking resemblance to the language used to justify occupation of the lands of aboriginal peoples in the Americas or Australia. Phrases like "empty lands," "new countries," and "the frontier" come to mind. One gets a strong sense of history repeating itself where wealthy outsiders visit their fantasies upon an economically handicapped people.

Small Sami tourism, fishing, and reindeer-herding companies have been started in reaction to the large-scale commercial fishing operations. However, these businesses are unable to compete with the large operators. Small-scale and ecologically sound tourism presents an excellent opportunity for the Sami to generate employment and industry in the changing economic climate of

A military tank yard on the Kirkenes-Murmansk road.

Russia. Until now, tourism development on the Kola Peninsula has featured exploitation of what were once traditional Sami lands and resources for the benefit of foreign investors and consumers. The most effective business assistance that the Sami could receive today would be the creation of small-scale joint ventures that combine foreign business skills with traditional Sami know-how in fishing, tourism, or herding.

Another major threat to Sami livelihood is the aggressive poaching of reindeer herds. There are essentially two types of poachers: those who poach for food, and those who poach purely for economic gain. The latter often have access to helicopters and are likely to be from the higher ranks of the military. They shoot indiscriminately into the herd, placing the herders at great personal risk.[12] Many of the younger animals, if not killed by indiscriminate shooting, are maimed in the stampede caused by the helicopter hunt.[13] In late 1996, a Komi reindeer herder near Loparskaya, married to a Sami women, encountered a poacher in his camp who demanded meat. The reindeer herder replied, "I have no meat." The poacher then suggested that

---

[12] Reindeer herders say that when they see poachers, they run away, often abandoning their snowmobiles and other equipment.

[13] Bullets have often been found in reindeer when they are slaughtered.

they share a drink. The reindeer herder accepted a drink from the poacher and soon after passed out. He awoke to find that the poacher had put water into his boots and his feet were frozen. The doctors now report that both his legs have been amputated (Leif Rantala, pers. comm.). Given these conditions in which the market system is pressing itself upon the lives of the Sami and their neighbours, the collapsed Communist regime looks increasingly more appealing. Growing frustration is causing some reindeer herders to find new merit in the old, repressive regime. "I am a supporter of strong laws," argues Nikolai Lukin. "We need to get some kind of laws." The basis of his support has little to do with an understanding of Communist policies, but reveals a desire for some central authority to govern and re-establish the rule of law.

The Sami small business of reindeer husbandry has made some positive strides. There were two state farms under the old Communist regime: Tundra and Lenin's Memorial. The Tundra State Farm has been privatized, and a Sami woman, Olga Anufrieva, is president. However, privatization has its perils in a context where the memory of family or individual ownership of herds has been significantly erased as a result of Communist oppression. A Swedish company, Norrfrys, has now established a slaughterhouse in Lovozero. The Tundra Company sells all of its meat to this company. In effect, this means that the best-quality meat goes abroad, and little meat remains for the local market. Today there is also little fuel to heat Sami houses. While G. Loomis Outdoors Adventure has plenty of hot running water in its camp, the town of Lovozero can provide hot water to only half of its homes.

Across the Finnish and Norwegian borders of the Kola Peninsula, western Sami herders are bracing themselves for a modern-day gold rush, as mining firms are poised to undertake exploration and development in Norway, Finland, and Sweden. The Sami fear they will lose the rights over their traditional land to these mining companies. It will not be long before the mining activity spills over into Russia.

It is worthwhile to consider the implications of the collapse of the Soviet empire and the rise of the market system for the Sami, Nenets, Komi, and Russians alike. The fall of the Iron Curtain has released valuable human and financial resources on both sides that were once engaged, at a dogmatic level and with religious ferocity, in mutual belligerence. These resources can now be devoted to other causes, such as community development. However, the decline of Communist dogma has also released us from viewing capitalism with rose-tinted glasses. We can see the market system for what it is: a human construct with weaknesses and strengths. As the inhabitants of the Kola peninsula struggle with the market system, we should keep in mind that workers have not been paid for almost a year; poaching of their reindeer herds is increasing; law enforcement is declining; large sectors of society are dispossessed; and citizens are "free" to be hungry and homeless. In many respects, the current situation mirrors their colonization in the early part of this century. We have learned little over the past hundred years.

A memorial minus Joseph Stalin in Lovozero.

CHAPTER 11
THE DREAM OF IMPLEMENTING
CO-MANAGEMENT IN THE KOLA PENINSULA

With maps completed and the concept of co-management oft discussed, we are now embarked on plans for a new era of land-use planning in the Kola Peninsula. We are taking small, practical steps in this implementation process, mindful that it took over 40 years to legally establish the concept in the Canadian western Arctic (Roberts, 1996:3). In Canada, the first step was to form local hunters and trappers committees that would meet with government representatives to discuss mutual resource management. In this way local concerns slowly began to influence resource planning and allocation activities. While the pace was slow, the persistence was provided by the aboriginal people, in the Canadian case by the Gwich'in and the Inuvialuit of the Mackenzie delta region. Whenever government officials backtracked, or forgot, or lacked resolve, it was the trappers and hunters of Aklavik and Fort McPherson who kept up the pressure in the cause of co-management. We see no reason why co-management regime development in the Kola will go any faster; we also see the need for the same qualities of tenacity and persistence.

Karim-Aly and Mike with their landlady and cook Genya in Lovozero, July 1997.

We must also proceed in the Kola mindful of the recent history of 70 years of state Communism, and of the prior rule of the Czars. As John Hall recently commented, both czarism and bolshevism conspired to destroy civil society in Russia (Hall, 1995:22-23). Ironically, as our experience indicates, unchecked capitalism with its ethos of rampant individualism also threatens civil society. The absence of a strong tradition of self-organization and voluntarism is strongly felt in Murmansk County, where the Duma officials still refer to the Kola Sami Association as an unofficial organization. Even in the new economic era, old traditions continue, and they strongly resist the growth of civil society bodies like co-management committees that (at least initially) draw their legitimacy from ideal rather than statute, and from voluntarism rather than corporate or government employment. In arguing for co-management in modern Russia, we are not just advocating the inclusion of traditional environmental knowledge in decision making about use of resources; we are really starting with the notion of creating institutions of civil society in a state characterized by their absence.

A more Russian approach to the problem of creating a Kola co-management regime may lie in the pioneering work of Dmitry K. Solov'ev, the father of multipurpose nature reserves (Solov'ev, 1920). Povrovskaya (1997:3) notes that Solov'ev introduced the concept of the multipurpose protected area and really anticipated the concept of the biosphere reserve, which was first discussed 51 years later at the inaugural conference of the United Nations Man and Biosphere Program. Solov'ev advocated a Siberian land-use regime comprising an absolutely untouched central zone to act as an animal nursery area; a secondary area within which limited hunting could occur; and a tertiary so-called "Karagas Territory" (named after the Karagas tribe, a small indigenous people of Siberia) for the purpose of cultural survival. Interestingly, the Karagas (whose modern name is Tofalars) are reindeer herders and hunters, who pursue a nomadic lifestyle linked to "vertical and short" reindeer migrations (Povrovskaya, 1997:3). Solov'ev's arguments for setting aside "Karagas territories" are apt today:

> Pointing in my preliminary report to the absolute necessity
> for the management of the definite inviolable territory for
> Karagas's nomadic lifestyle and hunting areas, I am taking

into account some reasons. There is a great difference between Russian and Karagas hunters. There are many variants for the Russians to change way of life, if the hunting resources would decline. But the existence of resources, especially sable and muskdeer (*Moschus moschiferus*), is the matter of life and death for the Karagas. Dying under the too close and sharp contacts with the Russians, the Karagas cannot live without taiga and sable, mountains and muskdeer, and *belogor'e* (high mountain areas) with the pastures for reindeer. It is absolutely impossible to reconcile ourselves to the perspective of extinction of the whole tribe, despite their small number, in the Russian Empire (1920).

Simply put, why should the Sami in 1998 not have the benefit of a core area, a buffer zone, and a transition zone for the maintenance of their reindeer and their culture in the Kola Peninsula? In this system, the reindeer calving areas could be given the highest level of protection, migratory corridors the next, with some allowance for controlled hunting and fishing, and the lowest level of protection would be afforded to the gathering and trapping areas that contribute to cultural sustenance and continuity. The Jona and Lovozero region maps are well suited to these land-use zone selection tasks; in fact, appropriate selections could be made by the mapping teams in a matter of days, if not hours.

Given that the political lobby for co-management must now primarily rest with the Sami themselves, the following actions have been taken to prepare for substantive negotiations with the Murmansk County Duma officials. At the conclusion of the mapping of the Jona and Lovozero Sami homelands in 1996, we held a series of short workshops to discuss how the maps would best be used to facilitate co-management. From the outset, it was decided to preserve the maps in the offices of the presidents of the Sami Associations of the two villages. A second set of maps (copies) were taken back to Canada for safekeeping, and to aid in the production of the book. Both Associations also agreed to appoint the local members of two provisional Sami Environmental Screening Committees (SESCs). It was seen to be important that the SESCs have a small majority of Sami members, a neutral chairperson, and membership from the relevant County authorities. The SESCs at the most basic level could function with two Sami delegates, a chairperson, one County official, and one local (municipal) official.

It was understood that the SESC would have an advisory role to the senior elected Murmansk County Duma politician with approval-granting authority for regional industrial development. This is the process followed in Canada, for example, by both the Inuvialuit Environmental Impact Screening Committee and the Environmental Impact Review Board, in their reporting relationship to the federal Minister of Indian Affairs and Northern Development.

The task of each SESC would be to screen all proposals for natural resource and industrial development in the Sami homelands to predict potential impacts on reindeer calving or migration, historic and sacred sites, and important natural resource harvesting areas. If negative impacts seemed likely as a result of the proposed development, the SESC would recommend mitigative measures to the County authorities. The SESC would also have the authority to refer proposals back to project proponents with requests for more specific information needed to better understand potential impacts

The primary tools of the SESC would be the detailed traditional land-use and occupancy maps. In the absence of GIS maps (and the ability of GIS to manipulate digital data, scales of display, and the use of colour), the proponent would be expected by the SESC to place the proposed project accurately on the 1:200,000 scale maps, using a sheet of plastic overlay. While every effort was made during the mapping process to obtain accurate, up-to-the-day (if not up-to-the-minute) information, the maps are to be considered open to the addition of new information, and to further validation and correction of existing information.

The potential of creating a Kola co-management regime was significantly reinforced on July 9, 1997, when the Canadian and Russian partners met with the mayor of Lovozero, Mr. Nikolai Brylov, and on July 10, when they met with a contingent of senior administrators and politicians, led by Vice-Governor Vasili Kalaida, and County Duma representative Galina Andreeva in Murmansk. The mayor became the first elected government official to see and review the maps, and he spoke candidly of their local utility after thinking initially that they contained only fishing and hunting information from the

1930s and 1940s. Key to his appreciation of the maps was their validation of his local environmental knowledge. As an avid hunter and fisherman, he is extremely concerned about the impact of new and proposed roads into the tundra and woodlands. "Such easy access will end it all..." he mused upon seeing the broad display of fish, fowl, big game, and berries on the Lovozero maps. This meeting in the Lovozero administration building concluded with a request by the mayor for copies of the maps for his office, and general supportive comments for the work to date.

The meeting held in Murmansk on July 10, 1997 saw 19 people assemble in a boardroom of the Administration of the County of Murmansk Building. Vice-Governor Kalaida chaired the two-hour meeting, which ran from 11 a.m. to 1 p.m. The maps for both Lovozero and Jona were presented by a team comprising Nina Afanas'eva, Larisa Avdeeva, Tat'yana Tsmykailo, Karim-Aly Kassam, and Mike Robinson. Listening and viewing with rapt attention were senior officials of the Kola Science Centre; the County Cultural Department; the Agricultural Sector; the Unofficial (non-governmental) Organizations Department; the Chairperson of the Committee of Natural Resources; the Assistant to the Deputy Governor; Ms. Galina Andreeva, the Chairperson of the Committee on Science, Education, Culture, and Nationalities; and four members of the Murmansk print and television media.

In his opening remarks, Mr. Kalaida, an official with wide experience in working with Small Peoples[14] from the Chukotka peninsula to the Murmansk region, centred the meeting on information exchange and the concept of co-management. It was not a meeting for decision making. Clearly he had been well briefed, and was ready for substantive discussions. Mr. Robinson opened the briefing with an overview of co-management in Canada and the development parallels which suggested its value to Russia and the Kola Peninsula. Nina Afanas'eva described the project partnership, and the selection of Lovozero and Jona as the participant communities. Karim-Aly Kassam, Larisa Avdeeva, and Tat'yana Tsmykailo next described the community work and their resulting maps. The methodology of mapping was carefully described, so that the participatory community approach was well

---

[14] "Small Peoples" is the generic Russian expression for northern aboriginal peoples.

understood. As Larisa noted, "This is how we got such high-quality information."

After their presentation, the project partners answered questions from the audience. Mr. Kalaida began with a general query relating to the lack of ethnic Russian, Komi, and Nenets information on the maps. Mr. Robinson replied that the maps were indeed open to the addition of other forms of local knowledge. He gave an example of cooperation in this task in Canada, where Dene Indians, non-aboriginal government officials, and regional tourism operators had combined their efforts in the western Arctic to produce a fine co-management map. Larisa Avdeeva cited recent discussions with Komi and Nenets people, which revealed their information was already part of the Sami maps because of the long-established tradition of cooperative herding by Sami, Komi, and Nenets herders. Key support for the establishment of a co-management regime was provided by Mayor Brylov of Lovozero, when he took the podium to affirm the quality of the maps and point out the need to use this kind of information to protect local and regional resources for all Russians. Mrs. Evgenija Patsia, a former journalist and current researcher at the Kola Science Centre who has written on industrial development of the Kola Peninsula and the growth of ethnic identity among the Kola Sami, pointed out that similar maps have been made in Russia, in Yakutia, but never before in the Kola. Mrs. Andreeva went on to add that she had seen the Arctic Institute's community partners in Canada with her own eyes, and also saw the similarity in their need to include cultural data in project planning. She also complimented the project partners on their good work.

In his concluding remarks, Mr. Kalaida stated that "the State has not served the Sami well, and our next steps must be concrete and pragmatic." He mused aloud about the need for a possible County legislative enactment for the maps, to ensure that the map details would be publicly held and to make their use compulsory in national planning for development.

> Concerning co-management, I agree with Nina Afanas'eva.
> Natural resources are meant for everybody, taking account
> of traditional places of the Small Peoples. These places have
> to be separated in another way, than previously done in
> Russia.

He also complimented the project workers as follows: "I acknowledge and respect those who made these maps."

Buoyed by the tone of this meeting, the project workers began to prepare for more detailed discussions with both Lovozero and County officials. It seems that there may be a new openness in Murmansk County to inclusion of local and traditional knowledge in resource use planning. New supporters for the Sami cause include an important regional mayor and the County's vice-governor. It is time to put the Kola co-management process together from the grass roots up, and the Sami have clear and practical recommendations for action.

Federally, the Sami Co-Management Project still seeks ratification by the Russian Duma of the Land Act and the Act on the Status of Northern Aboriginal People, both of which will support Article 69 of the Constitution of the Russian Federation, adopted by referendum on December 12, 1993:

> The Russian Federation guarantees the rights of indigenous small peoples according to the universally-recognized principles and norms of international law and international treaties of the Russian Federation.

Until the two Acts are ratified, it will be impossible for the two Sami reindeer companies to obtain grazing leases for longer than 25 years. Under the terms of the current leases, the companies must pay rent after an initial five-year grace period. Rental payments for the final 20 years are so high that the companies may have to forfeit their leases. These requested ratifications may also make possible the creation of new, federally controlled protected areas on the model originally proposed by Solov'ev, and later promoted by the United Nations Educational, Scientific and Cultural Organization (UNESCO) as the Man and Biosphere Program, demonstrating the sustainable use goals of the World Conservation Strategy. Such an achievement would not only help the Russian Sami retain their homelands and their traditional connection to the reindeer; it would also showcase the theoretical contributions of Dmitry Solov'ev, Russia's father of the multipurpose protected areas concept.

Finally, the Kola Sami wish to establish a Russian Co-Management

Institute in Lovozero, where members of the other 48 aboriginal groups in Russia can come for training in co-management and to view the practice of co-management at first hand. If this part of the Sami dream can become a reality, the process of co-management may spread across the Russian North, community by community, as the people progressively map how they use their land and work to ensure that their traditional environmental knowledge is always considered in the process of making decisions about natural resource development. While this wish may now seem distant, the Sami of Jona and Lovozero know that they have taken the first steps on the road to its fulfillment.

REFERENCES

Arctic Circular, The. 1952. Conference on Eskimo Affairs. The Arctic Circular 4(4):41-43.

Bäck, Lennart. 1996. Saami and Scandinavians: Natural Resource Competition in the Swedish Reindeer Herding Region. In: Wheelersburg, Robert P., ed. Northern Peoples Southern States: Maintaining Ethnicities in the Circumpolar World. Umeå (Sweden): CERUM [Centre for Regional Science]. 183-211.

Berkes, Fikret. 1985. The Common Property Resource Problem and the Creation of Limited Property Rights. Human Ecology 13(2):187-208.

Brice-Bennett, C., ed. 1977. Our Footprints Are Everywhere: Inuit Land Use and Occupancy in Labrador. Nain, Newfoundland: Labrador Inuit Association.

Brody, H. 1981. Maps and Dreams. Vancouver, British Columbia: Douglas and McIntyre.

Campbell, Tracy. 1996. Aboriginal Co-Management of Non-Renewable Resources on Treaty or Traditional Territory. M.A. Thesis, The University of Calgary, Committee on Resources and Environment.

(Constitution Act) Canada. Constitution Act, 1982.

Dickerson, Mark O. 1992. Whose North? Political Change, Political Development and Self-Government in the Northwest Territories. Vancouver, British Columbia: University of British Columbia Press.

Freeman Research Ltd. 1976. Report: Inuit Land Use and Occupancy Project. Canada. Department of Indian Affairs and Northern Development (sponsor). Ottawa: Supply and Services Canada.

Gaski, Harald, ed. 1997. Sami Culture in a New Era: The Norwegian Sami Experience.

Glavin, Terry. 1996. Dead Reckoning: Confronting the Crisis in Pacific Fisheries. (David Suzuki Foundation Series) Vancouver, British Columbia: Greystone Books.

(Gwaii Haanas Agreement) 1993. Government of Canada and Council of the Haida Nation. Gwaii Haanas Agreement. Haida Gwaii and Ottawa.

(Gwich'in Final Agreement) 1992. Canada. Department of Indian Affairs and Northern Development. The Gwich'in Final Agreement. Ottawa: Department of Indian Affairs and Northern Development.

Haetta, Odd Mathis. 1996. The Sami: An Indigenous People of the Arctic. Translated by Ole Petter Gurholt. Karasjok (Norway): Davvi Girji O.S.

Hall, John A., ed. 1995. Civil Society: Theory, History and Comparison. 2nd ed. Cambridge (England): Polity Press.

(Inuvialuit Final Agreement) 1984. Canada. Department of Indian Affairs and Northern Development. The Inuvialuit Final Agreement. Ottawa: Department of Indian Affairs and Northern Development.

(James Bay Cree Final Agreement) 1978. Department of Indian Affairs and Northern Development. The James Bay Cree Final Agreement. Ottawa: Department of Indian Affairs and Northern Development.

Kalstad, Johan Klemet. Aspects of Managing Renewable Resources in Sami Areas in Norway. In: Gaski, Harald, ed. Sami Culture in a New Era: The Norwegian Sami Experience. Karasjok (Norway): Davvi Girji O.S. 109-126.

Kaminsky, Vasili I. 1996. Medical Care of the Indigenous Peoples in the Lovozero County. In: Seurajärvi-Kari, Irja, and Kulonen, Ulla-Maija, eds. Essays on Indigenous Identity and Rights. Helsinki: Helsinki University Press.

Kaplinsky, Raphael. 1990. The Economies of Small. London: Intermediate Technology Publications.

Kassam, Karim-Aly. 1994. Breaking The Barriers: A Background Paper for the Sahtu Education Symposium. Calgary: Arctic Institute of North America.

Kazakevitch, Olga A. 1997. Intercultural Education in the Areas of Indigenous Minority Populations: Problems and Perspectives. A paper of the Research Centre of Ethnic and Language Relations, Institute of Linguistics of the Russian Academy of Sciences, Moscow.

Lapin Kansa (newspaper). April 12, 1997. Rovaniemi (Finland).

Lasko, Lars-Nila. 1994. FoU-projekt om samerna. Diedut nr. 6. Alta (Norway): Saami Instituhtta.

Leach, Edmund R., ed. 1967. The Structural Study of Myth and Totemism. London: Tavistock Publications Limited.

Leems, Knud. 1767. Beskrivelse over Finmarkens Lapper: Deres tungemaal, levemaade og forrige afgudsdyrkelse. Copenhagen: Kongel. Waeysenhuses Bogtrykkerie.

Lévi-Strauss, Claude. 1955. The Structural Study of Myth. Journal of American Folklore 68:428-43.

Louk'yanchenko, Tat'yana. 1983. The Burial Customs of the Kola Samis.

Scandinavian Yearbook of Folklore 39:201-214.

———. 1994. The Russian Sami. In: Narody Rossii. Moscow.

Murmansk Region Committee of Statistics. 1995. Murmansk Region in Figures. Helsinki: Statistics Finland.

(Nisga'a Treaty Negotiations) 1996. Government of Canada, the Province of British Columbia, and the Nisga'a Tribal Council. Nisga'a Treaty Negotiations: Agreement-In-Principle. Ottawa.

North, Richard D. 1991. Arctic Exodus: The Last Great Trail Drive. Toronto: Macmillan of Canada.

Notzke, Claudia. 1994. Aboriginal Peoples and Natural Resources in Canada. North York: Captus University Publications.

(Nunavut Final Agreement) 1995. Canada. Department of Indian Affairs and Northern Development. The Nunavut Final Agreement. Ottawa: Department of Indian Affairs and Northern Development.

Povrovskaya, Irina V. 1997. Nature Protected Areas and Indigenous Societies and Cultures: Mutual Advantages of Cooperation. Unpublished paper on file at the Institute of Geography, Russian Academy of Sciences, Moscow, and the Arctic Institute of North America, Calgary.

Rantala, Leif. 1995. The Russian Sami Today. In: Bjørklund, Ivar, Møller, Jakob J., and Reymert, Per K., eds. The Barents Region. Tromsø (Norway): University of Tromsø. 56-62.

Rasmussen, Hans-Erik. 1995. The Sami in the Kola Peninsula. In: Bjørklund, Ivar, Møller, Jakob J., and Reymert, Per K., eds. The Barents Region. Tromsø (Norway): University of Tromsø. 48-55.

Roberts, Karen E. 1994. Co-management: Learning from the Experience of the Wildlife Management Advisory Council for the Northwest Territories. Unpublished master's thesis. The University of Calgary, Faculty of Environmental Design.

———, ed. 1996. Circumpolar Aboriginal People and Co-management Practice: Current Issues in Co-management and Environmental Assessment. Calgary, Alberta: Arctic Institute of North America and Joint Secretariat - Inuvialuit Renewable Resource Committees.

Robinson, Mike, Janvier, Stuart, Herman, Elmer, and Garvin, Terry. 1993a. Traditional Land Use and Occupancy Study: Janvier and Chipewyan Prairie: Final Report. Fort McMurray, Alberta: Athabasca Native Development Corporation. Manuscript on file at the Arctic Institute of North America, Calgary, Alberta.

Robinson, Mike, Poelstra, Lena, and Garvin, Terry. 1993b. Traditional Land Use and Occupancy Study: Conklin Settlement: Final Report. Fort McMurray, Alberta: Athabasca Native Development Corporation. Manuscript on file at the Arctic Institute of North America, Calgary, Alberta.

Robinson, Mike, Garvin, Terry, and Hodgson, Gordon. 1994. Mapping How We Use Our Land Using Participatory Action Research. Calgary, Alberta: Arctic Institute of North America.

(Sahtu Final Agreement) 1994. Canada. Department of Indian Affairs and Northern Development. The Sahtu Final Agreement. Ottawa: Department of Indian Affairs and Northern Development.

Sami Instituhtta. 1990. The Sami People. Karasjok (Norway): Sami Instituhtta.

Sarv, Marju. 1996. Changes in the Social Life of the Kola Sami. In: Seurajärvi-Kari, Irja, and Kulonen, Ulla-Maija, eds. Essays on Indigenous Identity and Rights. Helsinki: Helsinki University Press.

Savio Art Museum, Kirkenes. 1993. John Andreas Savio: An Exhibition of his Selected Works in Texas, Washington and Alaska. Preface by Rami Abiel. Kirkenes (Norway): Savio Art Museum.

Solov'ev, Dmitry K. 1920. Sayansky Trade-Hunting Region and its Sable Trade. Ser. 2 Sayanskaya Expedition, GIZ. (in Russian).

Svonni, Mikael. 1996. The Future of Saami - Minority Language Survival in Circumpolar Scandinavia. Northern People, Southern States: Maintaining Ethnicities in the Circumpolar World. Umeå (Sweden): CERUM [Centre for Regional Science]/Umeå University.

Usher, Peter J., and Noble, G. 1975. New Directions in Northern Policy Making: Reality or Myth? Inuvik, Northwest Territories: Committee for Original Peoples' Entitlement.

Vattenkraften och rennäringen. 1986. Solna (Sweden): Vattenfall.

Volkov, Nikolai N. [1946] Translation by Lars-Nila Lasko and Chuner Taksami, 1996. The Russian Sami: Historical-Ethnographic Essays. Kautokeino (Norway): Nordic Sami Institute.

INDEX